𝕯ante 𝕽evisited

‖ ♥ ‖ ♥ ‖ ♥ ‖ ♥ ‖ ♥ ‖ ♥ ‖ ♥ ‖ ♥ ‖ ♥ ‖ ♥ ‖ ♥ ‖ ♥ ‖ ♥ ‖ ♥ ‖ ♥ ‖ ♥ ‖

ESSAYS
by
ANNE PAOLUCCI

‖ ♥ ‖ ♥ ‖ ♥ ‖ ♥ ‖ ♥ ‖ ♥ ‖ ♥ ‖ ♥ ‖ ♥ ‖ ♥ ‖ ♥ ‖ ♥ ‖ ♥ ‖ ♥ ‖ ♥ ‖ ♥ ‖

WITH A SPECIAL ESSAY ON THE OCCASION OF THE 700TH
ANNIVERSARY OF DANTE'S BIRTH BY

DINO BIGONGIARI

DA PONTE PROFESSOR EMERITUS
COLUMBIA UNIVERSITY

Publisher's Cataloging-in-Publication Data

Paolucci, Anne

    Dante revisited : essays / by Anne Paolucci ; with a
special essay on the occasion of the 700th
anniversary of Dante's birth by Dino Bigongiari —
1st ed. — Middle Village, NY : Griffon House
Publications, c2008.

    p. ; cm.

    ISBN: 978- 1-932107-24- X
    includes bibliographical references

    1. Dante Alighieri, 1265-1321—Criticism and
interpretation. 2. Dante Alighieri, 1265-1321.
Divina commedia. I. Bigongiari, Dino. II. Title.

PQ4390 .P286 2008
851. 1–dc22   0805

II ♥ II ♥ II ♥ II ♥ II ♥ II ♥ II ♥ II ♥ II ♥ II ♥ II ♥ II ♥ II ♥ II ♥ II ♥ II ♥ II ♥ II

GRIFFON HOUSE PUBLICATIONS
P. O. Box 790095
Middle Village, New York 11379
Tel.: (718) 821-3916; FAX: (718) 821=3916 (*51))

CONTENTS

This book is dedicated to
DR. FRANK D. GRANDE,
scholar, beloved teacher, loyal friend

AUTHOR'S NOTE

Shortly before his sudden and untimely death on Thanks-giving Day 2006, Dr. Frank Grande, President of Griffon House Publications and for many years Chairman of the History Department of the City College of The City University of New York — a long-time colleague and treasured friend — urged me to bring together a number of my writings, published over the years in academic and other journals. He felt that they should be accessible in book form and suggested, in particular, my scattered essays on Dante. His prodding was the impetus I needed to produce this volume.

Included, as an introductory essay, is a most interesting manuscript I happened to find in the materials left to me and my husband by Dino Bigongiari, the eminent Dante scholar, Da Ponte Professor at Columbia University for several decades, and our mentor and friend during the late 1950s and early 1960s. The piece was obviously written at the request of scholars, archivists, and government officials of Florence, who were preparing for celebrations to commemorate in 1965 the 700th anniversary of the birth of their most eminent citizen.

The piece was very likely meant to be a lecture and carried no title (I provided one). Whether it actually was delivered or was meant for publication in one of the commemorative programs is not clear, but it came into my hands at an opportune time; in fact, finding it was a major factor in my decision to take up Dr. Grande's suggestion. I placed it at the beginning of this volume, as a brilliant opening and the measure of perfection which the rest of us must try to live up to.

ANNE PAOLUCCI
February 4, 2008

THE MAN AND THE POEM

The essay which follows. by the renowned medieval and Renaissance scholar, DINO BIGONGIARI, *was probably written in anticipation of the commemorative celebrations of the 700th anniversary of Dante's birth (1265). The author had been invited to Florence to help sort out important manuscripts for projected displays. The text reproduced here was very likely prepared for a public lecture or perhaps for inclusion in a commemorative publication. The original copy did not carry a title.* [A.P.]

Two fundamental questions arise when we speak of Dante:

Is he a popular poet?
Is he a classic poet?

They are very different questions, stemming from opposite poles of the cultural horizon. The answers to these divergent questions, I hasten to add, need not themselves be divergent. Let's start with the first question.

In the last few months I've had vivid, not to say graphic proof of Dante's popularity, thanks to an experience which I consider a rare privilege, since it can have been shared by few others. In connection with the centenary celebrations, the Biblioteca Nazionale of Florence has been organizing an exhibit of manuscripts, documents and prints dealing with Dante. In the course of helping with this exhibit, I have examined hundreds of codices of the *Comedy* and especially those which are preserved in the precious Florentine libraries. The obliging clerks would bring them to my desk, sometimes ten at a time. I would hold in my hands a precious, richly miniatured copy of selected leaves of vellum, carefully ruled for the calligraphy of the expert copyist, and in the next moment, a rough copy, or at least a cheap one, jotted down on inferior paper in a rough businessman's hand, perhaps by a lay brother or a shopkeeper a step removed from illiteracy. In the transcription of the text, it frequently — indeed, usually — happens that the copyist from another region irregularly but quite consciously substitutes the characteristics of his own dialect for the grammatical form of Dante's "illustrious Florentine."

So, for example, in a manuscript from the Dominican convent of San Marco the several monks from various regions of Italy who took turns in writing it each added their particular dialectical veneer to the text: an Emilian writes *çongon* in place of *giungon,* while a brother from the Abruzzi gives *fando* for *fanno.* Another brother, this time from the Romagna, does not shy away from changing the words themselves, as well as the phonetics: where Dante writes *già sgorger puoi,* he writes *già pòi sgusir.* Moreover, dialectical and commercial variation intersect, as in the gem on display at the British Museum, the Yates Thompson codex, illuminated by two prestigious Sienese painters, the text of which betrays the speech characteristic of the border between Tuscany and Umbria. This, it should be noted, well into the fifteenth century, almost immediately before the standardization brought about by the invention of printing. Surprisingly enough, the physical appearance and layout of the page is subjected to the same variation. Sometimes there is simply the text, sometimes glosses in the margin, spilling over into the borders, sometimes interlinear notes as in a schoolboy's "pony" — all in the vernacular or even in Latin.

All of this clearly amounts to saying that men of all classes, regions and all degrees of culture have appropriated Dante, the supreme poet of the *Comedy,* to themselves — monks and shopkeepers, humanists and men of the upper middle-class, from Florence and from the center of Tuscany as well as the periphery and sometimes from beyond the Po and the Garigliano. Dante is the true, unifying bond among classes, climates, and regions. Our hands can touch on library shelves the force that was to become the father of his country.

So much for the popularity of the *Comedy.* But what of Dante's popularity beyond the confines of the work itself, without which he could not begin to be what he is? To this the legend of Dante bears witness, such as it is formulated, for example, in two famous short stories by a man of modest talent, Franco Sacchetti. A smith at his forge and a mule-driver transporting merchandise tend to their labors reciting, indeed murdering, Dante's verses. Obviously illiterate, they are therefore representative symbols of an oral tradition, within which we find elements of what specialists would refer to as "variant redactions": the smith, Sacchetti says, was "rummaging through his verses," "hanging and then mutilating them." Again, he has Dante say to the mule driver: "I didn't put that 'gee-up' in there."

As far as I am concerned, the testimony from Sacchetti is valid only insofar as it provides a precious record of a popular custom comparable to the singing of 19th century opera by humble people in the streets and the shops of Italy today. While I tip my hat to the smith and the mule-driver, active workers for the glory of Dante, I must reject Sacchetti's interpolation, which would have Dante break in, smashing tools, outraged at the massacre of his verses. In this detail I see a reflection of what a fashionable sociologist, Adorno, has called "half-culture," *halbkultur*, of which Sacchetti is an unbearable representative, obviously incapable of recognizing Dante's authentic wisdom, but equally incapable of grasping his true popularity, a popularity which sometimes involves paste-board figures, clashing colors and a long involved chain of precipitous rhyme; in short, a vocal repertory that one is tempted to compare with Verdi's.

If we examine our own consciences, we have to ask ourselves whether we still *read* Dante, and whether we read him not as an assignment or through a cultural sense of duty but simply as the result of a joyful decision to run through the whole story from one end to the other, conniving in the surprises prepared by the author, falling into his literary traps with a sense of collusion and delight. We do this at every moment when we re-read Homer and Virgil, Ariosto and Cervantes, Manzoni and Tolstoy, Proust and Joyce — is our experience the same when we read Dante's story? I don't think we can answer the question with an affirmative. The principle reason is that we cannot associate ourselves with the protagonist, the character who says "I" in the poem, and whose dual role has been illuminated by recent criticism, especially American criticism, as at once that of a specific individual and of humanity in general: "everyman," as Charles Singleton says. As for the action, the voyage of an Aeneas or the vision of a St. Paul can only be concluded successfully; salvation is assured. If I may use the words that I once heard spoken by a true poet and mystic, "The worst is over; the head of the mystical body is in heaven." Whatever uncertainty there is resides in the destiny of individuals, on whom the poet, usurping the privilege of God, passes judgment, revealing the ultimate and unknown fate of famous or at least impassioned human beings: "That which you cannot have heard," as Count Ugolino says; "the face which the pastor of Cosenza was not able to read in God," as Manfred says. The paralipomena on Francesca and Ulysses, on Buonconte and Piccarda, these are the discreet parts of the story which for us predominate over the story's continuity. Without a doubt, that continuity is far removed from us. In the modern world, even the most intentionally Christian of stories can draw its inspiration only from Christian ethics, rather than from Christian metaphysics. In short, Dante's continuity is his "libretto," subordinated to the prodigious execution of his music (and we shall see that this is not merely metaphor). That "libretto" is inspired by a culture whch is dated and extraneous to us, the culture over which, nevertheless, our philology labors ceaselessly every day.

Why then do we labor? Because a minute understanding of cultural presuppositions helps us the better to define and to measure the authentic Dante with respect to that which is not Dante. The far away quality of Dante's culture, of his "libretto," the book itself, is like the shadow against which the light is cast, the light, not of Dante's modernity but of something more: the eternal present of his poetry, recognizable in the continually surprising decisiveness of his speech, where imagination, like the rhythm of its genius, continually expands in order to recover itself once more. Dante's power is supreme, not in the continuity of his book but in the mere opening of it, or in our memory, which allows us to slow the pace as we will and to recognize anew the texture and weave of his words.

I cannot pretend to be exploring virgin territory in this discussion. The opposition of one Dante to another Dante inevitably recalls the outlines of the essay which Benedetto Croce dedicated to the *Poesia di Dante* on the occasion of the last centenary celebrations. This essay, the manuscript of which is in the possession of Yale, is worth more as a sincere and modern comprehension of the poetry, I dare say, than the whole tradition of scholarly exegesis put together. It does not matter that the so-called "lyrical" interpretation no longer corresponds to our contemporary preoccupations, or that the essay has provided professorial dialectics with a point of departure for boring legalistic exercises on the relationship of the two Dantes and on their supposed resolution into a unity. The distinction of "structure" and "poetry" is along the lines of the distinction proposed by German Romanticism between "system" and "poetry," which, in the work of Francesco De Sanctis, becomes a distinction between "intentional world" and "effective world" — but his considerable improvement was to make structure a necessary condition of poetry.

Whatever reservations one may have might better be directed against Croce's choice of images, which, because they are spatial, tend necessarily, by the very nature of language, to break down and separate the poetry into lyric and structural parts; whereas temporal and mathematical metaphors, with distinctions of the "continuous" from the "discreet" or of velocity make clearer, if I am not mistaken, the relationship between what is dated in Dante and what is eternal, somewhat like the distinctions between various "states" of matter, such as the liquid or the plastic states.

The four stars at the beginning of Purgatory enchanted Croce; they are immediately said to have been "non viste mai fuor ch'a la prima gente" {"never seen except by the first people"). This has the effect, at once, of going beyond the immediacy of pure spectacle. It should be understood that the enchantment felt by Croce results from a removal of the verse from its context, which is to say, it results from an apparently abusive critical process. Such an abusive process, whereby a definition of the classic is anticipated, can be used more or less throughout the whole poem. We shall see that the greatness or even the unity of Dante's poetry, an idea against which Croce never ceases to protest on theoretic grounds, can be found in its limitless capacity for translation into constantly shifting cultural terms, by virtue of which Dante has managed to survive the passionate interpretation of the romantics and the lyric interpretation of the historicists, to cite only recent hermeneutic schools, and remains open to a new type of reading, marked by the preceding ones, but perhaps more adapted to safeguarding the unity of the work.

Thus, the poetry of Dante resides less in the book and more in our memory of the poem. At first, this formula seems strange indeed when uttered by someone who is a philologist by profession and who, therefore, seems dedicated to an idolatry of the book. But if philology is unable to adapt itself to the specific nature of the objects of its study, so much the worse for philology. It is a fact nevertheless that, unless this paradox is mere metaphor, one should be able to trace its consequences even in the way that the poem has been transmitted to us. One cannot possibly pretend that the tradition of the *Comedy* is an oral tradition; nevertheless, it is not the sort of tradition that one can trace in the neat vertical family tree characteristic of poems handed down to us in a rational, written tradition. It would be unwise to dwell upon too many technical details on an occasion such as this; it will suffice to consider for a moment the case of ancient variants in the text, which are perfectly interchangeable, such as the verse concerning the glory of Virgil:

e durerà quanto il mondo [moto] lontana. . . .

(it will last as long as the world [motion of the world] lasts.)

Or, on the banks of the Acheron:

anche di quà nuova schiera [gente] s'auna.

(here too, another flock [people] is gathered).

Insofar as we deal with variants that are not the author's own, the fact that the range of such competing variants intersect with one another suggests that the scribes had at their disposal a whole spectrum of variants from which they might choose quite freely. This is true of all scribes and not simply of those who collated several manuscripts in order to attain some kind of critical edition.

It might be said in passing that an attentive study of all the variants in the poem, such as has already been begun for Dante's *Rime*, is a task that would be as rewarding as it is formidable. At any rate, it may be said that these variants in the manuscript tradition represent a kind of collective collaboration between the author and the memory of a whole nation for the making and the transmission of the text. A copyist, in fact, at best simply copies, but he also remembers (with variation, more or less exactly).

If anything, one might wonder that so instantaneous and enormous a diffusion of a text did not result in an even greater fragmentation — given the fact that we not only lack an autograph manuscript but even any manuscript derived from it within fifteen years of the poet's death, due most probably to the cheap quality of the paper that was used or, in other words, to the poverty of the environment in which the text was diffused. This amounts to saying that the authoritative quality of the style conferred a noteworthy stability to the text. In this manner, the consignment of the text to the national memory will appear as a function of the objective memorability of Dante's world.

It is at this point that we may finally ask ourselves: what does the word "classic" mean, when we apply it to Dante?

Dante has toward Virgil, the prince of poets, the same reverence that Statius later demonstrates. Dante calls upon his "lungo studio" and his "grande amore" of the *Aeneid*. Statius will say of Virgil's poem:

> la qual mamma
> fuori, e summi nutrice poetando

> (a mother to me
> it was and a nursemaid to my poetry).

Already in the *Vita Nuova* Dante had successfully claimed for the "rimatori," that is, for the poets of the vernacular, the prerogatives of the poets in Latin, the true "poets." Moreover, Dante's protesting disclaimer, "Io non Enea, io non Paolo sono" ("I am not Aeneas, I am not Paul"), means, on the contrary, that Dante will be both the inspired writer and the Virgil of his own situation. He begins, in fact, as a prophet, deliberately echoing Isaiah: "Ego dixit: In dimidio dierum meorum vadam ad portas inferi" and the association of the three beasts found in Jeremiah: "leo," "lupus," and "pardus"; all of which have meaning on several levels, in conformity with the "polysemous" or "multilevelled" quality of the Bible, of which Dante himself speaks. For thinkers of the Middle Ages, the *Aeneid* and the *Metamorphoses* were also susceptible of "polysemous" reading. Dante's filial feeling toward the *Aeneid* must however be understood on another level, that of worldly rhetoric. All of us have dissected the flowers of verse, culled from both meadows, the school of Dante as well as that of Virgil, and placed them side by side in our rhetorical herbals. This is not a totally useless scholarly pastime, but it fails to reach the heart of the matter.

The teaching of the classics is all in their authority, in their quotability, in the memorability of the words, in their character that is at once fresh and definitive. It is from a work that is classic that we are able to extract words that are unchangeable, words whose truth seems confirmed by our own unpublished experience. The classics, particularly the Latin classics, and Virgil most of all, seem to be characterized by the fact that they are at once tightly woven and yet capable of being cited in fragments that immediately yield a fullness of meaning. For example: "per amica silentia lunae" ("and for a friend, the silence of the moon"). In its context, the phrase has a tactical meaning: the weather is fitting for a military expedition. But those who sample the classic tradition remove it from its context and find in it a suggestion of a sentimental accord with nature, the participation in the enchantment of the night. The vitality of the classics consists precisely in this range of misuse, in this capacity to be translated in autonomous units of sense. And it is in this sense that Dante has become a classic in his own right.

A classic is a repertory of verse, a reservoir of what medieval men called the *auctoritates*, memorable sayings capable not only of embellishing but also of giving structure to human discourse. One might in fact make the point with one of Dante's own verses: "Parlan Bellezza e Virtù all'intelletto." ("They speak Beauty and Virtue to the intellect.") This is as eminently medieval as is the proposition that Beauty is the splendor of Truth. The modern reader, used to the geometric quality of rational exposition, is always surprised when he discovers that the great medieval treatises, the *summas*, are organized within a dialectical framework of a particular school, that is, within a sophistic tradition. Even for a man like Dante, the sources of knowledge are not only logical deduction and experimental induction but also, perhaps most of all, the wisdom of the whole human race that the "autori" (he says of Virgil, "tu se' lo mio maestro e 'l mio autore") have preserved for him precisely in the *auctoritates*, which thus take their place side by side with Holy Scripture as the transmitters of revealed truth. As example of *auctoritates*, we cite the words Francesca da Rimini quotes from one of Dante's "doctors," Boethius —

. . . Nessun maggior dolore
che ricordarsi del tempo felice
nella miseria. . . .

(no greater grief
than to remember happy days
in wretchedness. . . .)

But Dante himself, having been taught by the ancients, goes on to produce *auctoritates* of his own — memorable sentences of the type that in German are called "geflügelte Worte." With bold innovation, he intends to be a classic writer in the vulgar tongue, turned toward a public far more inclusive than the traditional "clerks" and "letterati." In so doing, he opens a new art era and at the same time brings it to a close. After him, there is no one who approaches the democratic, exemplary quality, at once literary and full of wisdom, that earns for Dante the title of "classic."

It would be instructive to rank the *auctoritates* contained in the *Divine Comedy*. One might begin with those elements that are purely traditional, as when, for example, he forces Virgilian hexameters, into hendeca-syllables through a zeal for rhyme, allowing expressive force to prevail over accuracy in translation:

Perchè non reggi tu, o sacra fame
dell'oro, gli appetiti de' mortali?

(Why do you not restrain, O sacred hunger
for gold, the appetites of mortals?)

One might then turn to a passage where he speaks purely with his own voice, without formal inspiration or syntactic distortion but with a nonetheless lapidary quality:

Lunga promessa con l'attender corto
ti farà trionfar nell'alto seggio.

(A long promise held for a short time
will make you triumph in the high seat.)

But we must bring these examples to a close, or our documentation would have to include the entire text, which, almost literally, exists in the memory of all Italians. This is to say nothing of the innumerable sentences that have become proverbial, from the "mezzo del cammin" to the "amor che muove il sole e l'altre stelle," still used with such frequency and such banality that they have become tedious. To limit ourselves only to the very first cantos, we have "selva selvaggia, "uscito fuor del pelagi alla riva," "falsi e bugiardi," "tremar le vene e i polsi," "qui si parrà la tua nobilitade," "color che son sospesi," "la vostra miseria non mi tange," "il ben dell'intelletto," "dentro a le segrete cose," "sanza infamia e sanza loco," "a Dio spiacenti ed a' nemici sui," "sciaurati che mai non fur vivi," "bianco per antico pelo." But just as etymology restores many metaphors which have slipped into common language back to their original freshness, so too, a slight effort suffices to reconstitute the originality of these images and turns of phrase to equal that of so many others which have not become worn with time and usage.

It is therefore memory upon which the energy and even the violence of Dante's speech is impressed, that links classic intention with popular impact. It is no wonder that the first to have exercised his memory on the text is Dante himself. We must now delve for a moment, as briefly as we can, into the philological laboratory, in order to demonstrate in what sense Dante remembers Dante.

It is relatively easy to compile a catalogue of stylistic devices used by any particular author. Such catalogues can then be used by scholars trying to make attributions, just as specific techniques can help to attribute works of art to particular artists. We shall see that the same sort of procedure has its usefulness in Dante scholarship as well. As any rate, in ordinary contexts, the repetition of specific words or figures of speech are connected to meaning, the semantic aspect of discourse. This is also true of the Dante within Dante of course, but there is nothing unusual about it. What is unusual is that certain echoes of Dante within Dante, or rather, of the *Comedy* within the *Comedy*, since the other works in the vernacular by Dante, especially Dante of the *dolce stilnuovo*, can be safely left out of this discussion, certain echoes of the work within the work differ greatly from those that can be found in the works of other writers imitating Dante, whether crudely as in the worst writing of Boccaccio, or accurately as in Monti's literary crafsmanship.

Why is it that to imitate Dante has proven to be so fruitless an undertaking while, to cite the opposite extreme, the imitation of Petrarch has seemed completely legitimate? The answer is that Dante's world — and this means above all his linguistic world — is above all *open*, from the beginning, while imitators naturally tend to regard that world as if it were closed. On the contrary, the world of Petrarch is highly selected, uniform and closed with respect to the life or development of the *dolce stil nuovo* and especially of the young Dante. If in a certain sense all has been said in Petrarch's poetry, then the internal evolution of the poetry itself and whatever additions that were brought to the *Canzoniere* by Petrarch's imitators affect only the order and grouping, not the substance. By definition, one imitates only the absolute and, in fact, imitation is the great humanistic and Renaissance canon of art. In Dante, there is no imitation. He emulates, not repeats, even the classics, as we have already seen. We have also seen that he both begins and ends the epoch of emulation in the vernacular, which is succeeded then by the epoch of imitation in Latin, as well as the vernacular.

Having established these premises, let us examine several by no means unrepresentative examples of echoes of the *Comedy* within the *Comedy* in order to draw some general conclusions. With the same method, we will establish two exceptions: first, an exception to the rule that only within the *Comedy* do we find an adequate echo of the *Comedy*; second, an exception to the other rule, that the *Comedy* really echoes only the *Comedy*. Both of the exceptions will have corresponding important implications.

When, at the beginning of the Purgatorio, Virgil justifies himself with Cato with the following lines:

> . . . da me non venni:
> donna scese dal ciel, per li cui preghi
> de la mia compagnia costui sovvenni.

> (I do not come on my own. A lady descended
> from heaven, by whose prayers I am
> helping this one with my guidance.)

The lines clearly evoke and reflect in the formal detail of the argument the justification of Dante to Cavalcanti:

> . . . da me stesso non vegno:
> Colui ch'attende là, per cui mi mena
> forse cui Guido vostro ebbe a disdegno.

(I do not come by myself alone; the one
who waits there to lead me through her [intercession]
whom, perhaps, your Guido held in disdain.)

If this *cui*, the object of the disdain, is, as most by now tend to believe, Beatrice, that lady links together by her personal identity two *terzine* which are syntactically so much alike. Further, she explains the presence of insertions which make the conjunction of Virgil and Cato parallel with that of Beatrice and Virgil at the beginning of the Inferno. Virgil says to Cato:

Grazie reporterò di te a lei [Marzia]

(I will bring back thanks to her [Marzia])

as Beatrice had said to Virgil:

di te me loderò sovente a lui [il Signore]

(I will praise you often to him [God])

and Cato to Virgil:

bastiti ben che per lei [Beatrice] mi richegge

(suffice it to say that for her you ask it of me)

as Virgil had already said of Beatrice:

tal che di comandare io la richiesi

(such that I asked her to command me).

The verbal similarity, whether spontaneous or calculated, might seem at first to be like so many others, a result of the thematic and conceptual similarity. But if we return again to the *terzina* with which we began, and precisely to the central verse which slides into the next by means of the relative introduced by the *per*,

donna scese dal ciel, per li cui preghi . . .

our memory infallibly recalls a totally difference *terzina* whose central verse is coordinated with a preceding hemistich that it clarifies before slipping into the subsequent verse:

elli stesso s'accusa;
questi è Nembròt, per lo cui mal coto
pur un linguaggio nel mondo non s'usa.

(he accuses himself;
this is Nembroth, because of whose evil thought
one language alone is not spoken in the world).

Is this the memory of the reader or is it not, above all, the memory of the writer, completely unrelated to the content and reflecting in the identity of form a sort of original organizational principle?

Almost every passage of the *Comedy* may be subjected to an analogous mnemonic breakdown into echoes of preceding passages and anticipations of successive passages. Such an exercise, which we do not have time to repeat here, defines the memory of Dante as not purely verbal, stimulated by similar circumstances in separate passages, but rather as constituted by rhythmic figures. Moreover, it is the function of the rhythm, in conformity with the dual nature of language, phonic and symbolic, to associate itself on the one hand with the intellectual line of the argument, reflected in the grammar and, on the other hand, with the tonal realization of the word. Ideally, if not statistically, the musical aspect predominates over the merely semantic or thematic in the list of Dantesque echoes of Dante.

It is understandable that a formula should be repeated in rhyme, that is, in a particular rhythmic phrase: for example, *caldi e geli* (in rhyme with *cieli* and with *si sveli* or *riveli*) is repeated in

a sofferir tormenti e caldi e geli

(to suffer torments of both hot and cold)

or in:

lievemente passava caldi e geli

(lightly endured hot and cold).

Even a rapid glance at a glossary of Dante's rhymes will reveal an infinite number of similar recalls: *mondo errante, andavan forte, di giro in giro, la virtù che vole, con sì dolce nota* (also in the plural), *tra cotanto senno* and who knows how many more. Also obvious are the repetitions of introductory formulas, such as *Ma dimmi, se tu sai, Non ti maravigliar (or non vi maravigliate) fannomi (or faccianli) onore . . . subitamente* and so on. It is much more significant, and surprising, to find that certain turns of phrase have a fixed rhythmic setting. When, for example, Guido Gozzano writes his famous verse in the poem Signorina Felicità,

Donna: mistero senza fine bello!

(Woman: beautiful mystery unending!)

which hendecasyllable of the *Comedy* does his *pastiche* resemble? Is it

per la tua fama sanza fine cupa

(because of your hollow hunger without end)

or

e sarai meco senza fine cive

(and you will be with me a citizen forever)

or again

giù per lo mondo senza fine amaro

(below in the world bitter without end)?

In all of these, *sanza fine* is placed before the final bisyllabic attribute or predicate. It is obvious that Gozzano is imitating no one verse but rather a figure, a rhythmic abstraction.

Another stunning rhythmic abstraction is the one that has the word *spesso* preceded by a word accented on the antepenultimate syllable, a proparoxytone: "una pegola spessa." Most often, in fact, it is a proparoxytone which contains a dental consonant:

[a cloud which is] lucida, spessa, solida e pulita

[a flash of lightning] subito e spesso a guisa di baleno,

and at the end of a verse:

una rena umida e spessa; . . . .

i vapori umidi e spessi; . . . .

[a wood] di spiriti spessi. . . .

It is quite evident here why we must speak of memory.

What semantic necessity would dictate the association of *spesso* with a proparoxytone, let alone one with a *t* or a *d*? Such a rhythmic-tonal synthesis is "arbitrary" or "unactivated," to use the terms of modern linguistics. But the felicitous combination must have struck the poet when first he invented it and then appealed to him, consciously or not, as something to be imitated.

The definitive proof of our interpretation is provided us by the verbal similarities between dissimilar or even antithetical contexts. The second realm, *il secondo regno,* which is repeated at the end of a verse, refers in one instance to Purgatory and in another to the heaven of Mercury. Again, Cacciaguida says of Can Grande, "notabili fien l'opere sue" ["his works will be noteworthy"] and our thoughts turn to Guido da Montefeltro: "l'opere mie non furon leonine, ma di volpe" ["my works were not of the lion but of the fox"], a comparison which, if it were deliberately intended, would be rather unflattering to Dante's distinguished patron and must therefore be ascribed to an involuntary memory. Or again,

per entro il cielo scese una facella,

which refers to sweet Gabriel, the Archangel; but a little earlier, we have

là onde scese già una facella,

which refers surprisingly to the evil tyrant Ezzelino. In the same manner we have

di quella spera ond'uscì la primizia,

that is, St. Peter; but certainly we see, thanks to memory, the rhyme between this *spera* and *schiera* in the verse

cotali uscir de la schiera ov'è Dido,

which refers no less to Paolo and Francesca. How much further can one go? The verse which makes God a point in the Empyrean,

sempre dintorno al punto che mi vinse,

reflects this very famous verse about the same sinners:

me solo un punto fu quel che ci vinse;

and shortly before,

quanti son li splendor a chi s'appaia,

said of the divine light, manifestly follows the verse concerning the she-wolf:

Molti son li animali a cui s'ammoglia.

These are limit-cases, from which there clearly emerges the predominance of what the Geneva school of linguistics would call the signifier over that which is

signified. There also emerges an even more general conclusion: if we accept the terms whereby De Sanctis contrasts Dante with Petrarch, the "poet" as opposed to the "artist," then an indisputable "poet" such as Dante reveals extreme formal characteristics that one might ordinarily consider characteristic of the pure "artist," such as Petrarch, who is nevertheless so much more "literary" than "musical" that formal characteristics of this kind are in him far less pronounced. From this point of view, Dante seems to be the only true heir of the *troubador* tradition of the poet-musician, even if he absorbs all of the melody into his entire verbal score. To be sure, the use to which we have put De Sanctis's distinction is motivated by a consideration totally different from his own. Not only does our use of the distinction not imply a choice between them, but it specifically rejects the possibility of such a choice, for we have transposed the antithesis "poet" and "artist" into an antithesis between the "inclusiveness" of Dante and the "exclusiveness" of Petrarch, vocations which are irreconcilable but of equal dignity and rank, between which it would be inconceivable to make a choice.

Nevertheless, Petrarch's echoes of Dante are precisely the surprising exception to the type of random citation to which Dante's text was to be subjected. Petrarch's echoes are rhythmic and melodic more than verbal, notwithstanding the ostentatious ignorance of Dante's poem that he displays in a famous defensive letter to Boccaccio. He praises Dante as a fine person, a friend of his father whom he once even met, but he denies any relationship to his poetry. Resemblances are accidental or the result of purely psychological coincidence. It is true that in disclaiming any debt toward his great co-citizen, Petrarch was practicing a totally legitimate kind of defense. A man whose mind was more exquisite than profound, addressing Boccaccio, a man of modest intelligence, Petrarch had to dissociate himself as much as possible from the "comic" Dante, that is, from the all-inclusive, understandable and tremendously versatile character of Dante's poetry. But insofar as he was called upon to answer a direct question, Petrarch ran the risk of perjuring himself — there are so many recalls in the *Canzoniere*, not only to the early Dante of the *rime* and the *petrose* but also to the *Comedy*. A scholar, forgotten today, Mascetta Caracci, listed many of them, both real and presumed. What interests us here, however, are those imitations which are rhythmic and phonic rather than verbal, resembling Dante's echoes of himself and thereby attesting to the almost involuntary quality of the recall. Of the massive number of instances, we cite only a few.

In a *ballata*, Petrarch writes,

conven che 'l duol per gli occhi si distilla
dal cor . . .

recalling, according to an excellent commentator, a passage of Dante's on the hypocrites:

ma voi chi siete, a cui tanto distilla
quant' i' reggio dolor giù per le guance . . .

and the reference of the verb *distillare* to *duol* or *dolore* is evident. But a less semantic and more subtle example is provided by a joyful passage on the beatific vision,

. . . ed ancor mi distilla
nel core il dolce . . . ,

more subtle perhaps but just as irrefutable, since the verb is also in rhyme and immediately preceding the complement *core*, before the *enjambement*. As far as the sense is concerned, the link between the passages is by no means necessary; they are joined only by rhyme. Hence the bond is vital rather than mental.

The beginning of a famous sonnet by Petrarch contains the following lines, which are essential for our next example:

I dolci colli ov' io lasciai me stesso . . .
mi vanno dinanzi; e èmmi ogni or a dosso
quel caro peso . . . .

Without much doubt, these lines recall another indelible memory — that of Mastro Adamo:

Li ruscelletti che de' verdi colli . . .
sempre mi stanno innanzi, e non indarno. . . .

The *colli* of the opening, whether *dolci* or *verdi*, the internal, marked by the relative, the verb with the word *dinanzi*, the *e* which follows, all serve to mark the thematic affinity with an identity of articulation.

Here again, a negative proof of the point is provided us by a case of contextual incongruity. When a verse describing Saint Anne in the Paradiso,

tanto contenta di mirar sua figlia,

provides Petrarch with one of his most famous verses,

Giove s'allegra di mirar sua figlia,

the variation would strike us as a profanation were it not for the fact that the purely emblematic mythology represents a reduction of reality, so vibrant in Dante's vision and imagination, into an arabesque of an international gothic. It is noteworthy; indeed it is the last time historically that a formalist of Petrarch's caliber can make use of Dante's phonic material, a sure sign of the inclusive and encyclopedic nature of Dante's temperament and of his polytonal range.

Now, for the second exception. The only writing in the vernacular, besides the *Comedy*, which seems to echo Dante as does the poem itself, is the *Fiore*. This conventional title covers a series of over two hundred sonnets found in a codex of Montpellier, which gives a resumé of the narrative portions of the *Roman de la Rose*. Many external details have convinced unprejudiced scholars that the excessive expressivity of these poems in the French style that might be called "burlesque-realistic" mark them as the work of the young Dante. But the queen of all proofs, scarcely utilized up until now by Basserman and De Robertis, is surely internal. It is scarcely possible that the author of the *Fiore* might constitute a third, independent personality to be ranked in the same expressive category with Dante and Petrarch.

I shall limit myself to Dante's echoes of himself. In a sonnet of the *Fiore*, "Pietà" is, together with "Franchezza," one of the ambassadors of the God of Love, which is a situation somewhat like Beatrice with Virgil at the beginning of the *Comedy*. At any rate, it seems to be underscored by coincidences of rhythm and timbre rather than words. The verse

> di non far grazia al meo domandamento

anticipates Virgil's reply to Beatrice,

> tanto m'aggrada il tuo comandamento.

A little further on,

> or avem detto . . .
> la cagion per che no' siam venuti,

as Virgil says to Dante,

> dirotti perch' io venni . . .,

while he says to Beatrice:

> ma dimmi la cagion che non ti guardi
> de lo scender qua giuso,

Immediately after, in the *Fiore*,

> molt' è crudel chi per noi non vuol fare!

which is equivalent in structure to Ugolino's words,

> ben se' crudel, se tu già non ti duoli.

It should be added that these comparisons between the *Comedy* and the *Fiore* are matched by comparisons that can be made between the *Fiore* and the *rime* of the *Vita Nuova*, or of about that time, while analogues between the *Comedy* and the *rime* are lacking or, at best, very rare. Which goes to prove that Dante "found himself" in the low and violently expressive style referred to as the "comic" style. Further, he found himself so thoroughly that he chose the name of that style for the title of his great poem. Thus, the *Fiore* represents a link in the chain that we would otherwise be unable to document.

I hope this three-fold, albeit brief excursion into the philological laboratory has at least indicated the experimental bases for a definition of Dante's robust and epigraphic voice, as capable as a classical quotation of being imprinted in our memories and indeed capable if activating Dante's own memory, through the periodic recurrence of rhythmic figures and words. If I am not mistaken, this demonstration serves somewhat to temper and to restrain that excessive taste for ideological interpretation of the poem, to which students of Dante feel themselves irresistibly inclined.

It occurs to ask at this point: to what is the memorability of Dante's poetry devoted? His imagination is such that every experience gives it incentive and stimulates its growth. Every element maintains its vigor, even when uprooted from its context and taken in isolation; nor is its individuality overwhelmed when it is surrounded by a multiplicity of elements. This in fact is the fascinating thing about Dante: on one hand, he will not admit poetic accumulation, the kind of super-abundance we consider characteristic of a baroque or neo-baroque poet; on the other hand, urged on by his task, his "alta vena," he leaves it to the reader to linger over the sublimity of particular details, while he continues along "from peak to peak," to use one of his own images.

The shifting climates of Dante's reality, its snow and its frost, its full moons and its horizons on the open sea trembling at dawn, together with his descriptions of animal life, his inexhaustible bestiary of fireflies, cranes, frogs and lions, show him to be a complete observer of nature, in immediate contact with daily basic occurrences within an ancient rural framework, marked only occasionally by some detail of a civic landscape (these fairly close to each other): the ring of towers surrounding Monteriggioni, the pine cone of Saint Peter's, the leaning Garisenda tower, etc.

But that great observer is a solitary figure, who, with a classical equanimity, pays attention not only to the external world but to the internal one as well; and of this interior world, not only is he intrigued by the mechanism of passion, the description of which so enraptured the romantic critics, but also by the operation of the intellect. Because of that operation, truth cannot be distinguished from the process of research, even when that research is incomplete or thwarted. So, for example, at the crowning moment of the poem, the geometer devoted to squaring the circle, who cannot find the principle he needs, "quel principio ond' elli indige"; the degree candidate who "s'arma e non parla," "who arms himself and does not speak," arms himself — please note

— not simply to answer the question but rather to establish it within the proper dialectic. It should in fact be noted that the veneer of scholastic teaching in the poem does not reflect a pedagogic dogmatism but rather represents a perpetual resolution of the truth in the mind of the scholar, in the role of pupil or in the role of teacher.

As a matter of fact, this historicity is not confined to learned quotations from the poem but also to natural descriptions. The marvelous summer scene,

> Quante il villan ch'al poggio si riposa
> vede ucciole giù per la vallea,
> forse colà dove vendemmia e ara,

> (As many fireflies as the peasant sees as he
> looks down from the terrace where he is resting,
> into the valley, perhaps where he harvests grapes or plows),

comes alive for us as well on Tuscan evenings, but it presupposes the condition of the Apennine valley in those days, when, at sunset, the peasant left the unsafe and unhealthy plain and withdrew under the protective cover of his quilt, away from the miasma and from the threat of highwaymen. At the same time, the bothersome insects of the stables make way for the equally annoying insects from the marsh, as Dante says in an aside: "Come la mosca cede alla zanzara" ("as the fly makes way for the mosquito"), powerfully oblivious to the formal rules about not distracting the reader with irrelevant details. I will not dwell on the fact that the historicity is specified as an implicit element of the poet's imagination. This is something familiar to us in modern writers. The posthumous memoirs of Hemingway reveal how he expected his readers to supply for themselves the fate of one of his characters, which he did not himself make explicit. This is an immanent sort of ellipsis, not of the type found in the canto of Francesca ("quel giorno più non vi legemmo avante") nor again of the Manzonian type ("la sventurata rispose") which admit of only one explicit interpretation, but rather of the type practiced in the *Vita Nuova* where, in one of his *canzoni* Dante says "mi volgo a parlare a indiffinita persona, avvegni che quanto a lo mio intendimento sia diffinita" ("I turn to speak to a person, it doesn't matter who, although I know who it is"). The most famous example of the principle occurs in what I am convinced is Count Ugolino's cannibalism, where he is forced by the "New Thebes" to eat of those heads, a situation used by Horace to exemplify the tragic situation. Again, the refutation of Averroism is accomplished by quoting in rhyme the "possible intelletto," which is also in rhyme in the great *canzone* of Guido Cavalcanti, "Donna me prega," that is, it tacitly but surely involves Guido himself in the refutation. Finally, why does Guido de Montefeltro compare himself and Boniface to Sylvester and Constantine, if not because both baptism and the donation of Constantine were the favorite themes of that Pope?

The historicity of Dante's nature can be brought into relief by comparing it with the usual artifice present in the Petrarchan patterns: "quel rosignol che sì soave piagne," and "e garrir preghe e pianger Filomena," which seems like byzantine or neogothic miniatures, outside of all geographic coordinates, eternal objects, platonic ideas. And one might continue the investigation, coming all the way down to Leopardi, in whose verse the sound of the frog "rimota alla campagna" separates itself from the moment in which it occurs to echo and endure within the soul, like the train whistle in Proust, bound up with a state of mind, while for Dante, constantly attuned to movement, the state of mind bursts forth instantaneously but does not solidify into permanence.

Furthermore, these epigrams drawn from the natural world which so delighted us with their decisive quality do not possess any formal autonomy. Fireflies, bachelors, geometers, etc. etc. are similes or metaphors introduced by "quale . . .," "quanto . . . ," "come . . .". Not content with remaining fixed there on the page to serve a subordinate purpose, they become as Chinese boxes, fitted with parentheses within parentheses and with incidental details that are not always relevant. Within the comparison of the peasant who contemplates the fireflies there is inserted not only an indication of time ("come la mosca . ..") but also the less explicit indication of the season:

quante il villan ch' al poggio si riposa
nel tempo che colui che' l mondo schiara
la faccia sua a noi tien meno ascosa . . .

so that, in order to isolate the simile it is necessary not only to remove it from the exterior context but also to trim it from within. But this kind of spatial isolation is relatively simple. It is the writing itself, as we were saying, that has two faces. A great verse such as the following would appear to have a certain immediacy:

la divina foresta spessa e viva.

In the light of its sublime context, the verse does not illustrate the joy of nature but rather a miraculous entity — as revealed by the word *divina*. Shortly before this, Dante extolled the vegetation "che qui la terra *sol da sè produce*" ("that the earth by itself produces"); further on, the crystal-clear water exceeds "l'acque che son *di quà più monde*" ("the waters that are purest here"), flowers bloom "senza seme" ("without seed"). One should add the numerous mythological references: Proserpine, Venus, Leander, as a confirmation of the function of mythology as a figural repository. In fact, the sacred world and the classic correspond and fuse, just as even the student textbooks of the Middle Ages claimed they should (Theodulus), and we reach the point where the line from Virgil, "manibus O date lilia plenis" rhymes with the words of the psalmist, "Benedicts qui venis." In order to remove any suggestion of a bifurcation between the two sources of knowledge, direct and cultural, popular and learned, the lizard and the phoenix are on the same structural plain, as are the peasant terrified of the frost and the prophet Elisha witness to the ascent of Elijah.

Reality is primary but generic with Petrarch, while for Dante it is exact but subordinate, or at least substantially indirect. If landscape as an end in itself tends toward estheticism, as it obviously does, then in a great writer it must be sketched with sobriety or, as is the case with Dante, it must be made incidental or contingent. The texture of a contingent "libretto," in which the inexhaustible faculty of representation is made to serve doctrine or the figurative narrative, gives a real guarantee of independence to the scenes, to such a degree that they gain for themselves in posterity a totally independent value. This is the nucleus of the relationship of "structure" and "poetry," but we have to understand the question in the light of the meaning of "liberty" in the Middle Ages.

Unlike its modern counterpart, the medieval concept of liberty is brought into being with an extraordinary amount of flexibility within the confines of an absolute security, authority or faith. Religious orthodoxy, like political orthodoxy, allows a surprisingly wide range of criticism or behavior, when compared with the Counter-Reformation or with absolutism. In the same way, a rigorously theocentric cosmology, ordered around a nucleus which is infinitely removed, admits an extraordinary amount of liberty to the construction of human intelligence and imagination, allowing doctrinal works, including Dante's, to ignore in their obvious structures the geometric rigor which we have grown used to since the enlightenment, allowing imaginative works to be free of the constraint of regularity espoused by the humanists, even if they were eventually to be subjected to a rather tight rein, "fren dell'arte," not predictable *a priori*. Dante's world, which is neither the world of the humanists nor of the enlightenment, is therefore perpetually open to reality, a reality which is never unrelated, homogenous with a total culture and, as the banality would have it, encyclopedic.

The almost biological secret of Dante's experimental richness consists in his equally intense participation in, and even in his successive identification with, all objects in a way that is perfectly clear to his consciousness:

qual mi fec' io che pur da mia natura
trasmutabile son per tutte guise!

(and I became transmutable in my nature
in all [possible] ways).

An analogous disposition to metamorphosis explains the competition with Ovid ("Taccia di Cadmo e d'Aretuse Ovidio") which is also made explicit only when it is projected onto a more modest descriptive plain. It is striking to trace the progression of the *Vita Nuova* in terms of "transmigration" or "transfiguration" with which Dante established the precedent that made possible the Petrarchan *canzone* of metamorphosis. Dante is transfigured through Beatrice at the wedding feast in the episode of the "gabbo," when, as the sonnet "Con l'altre donne" stated, he assumed a "figura nova" — "mi cangio in figura d'altrui" ("I change into the shape of someone else"). Again, he was transformed by tears at the news of Beatrice's grief for her father. The *Vita Nuova* might be described quite literally as Dante's novel of transfiguration, while the *Comedy* is the hyperbole, pushed beyond the normal confines of human nature,

transumanar significar *per verba*,
non si poria

(to go beyond the human
cannot be signified in words),

where, again, the reference is, as usual, to one of the Ovidian metamorphoses — Glaucus transformed by tasting the grass — "nel gustar dell'erba." The transformation is boldly stated, but in an exterior way; however, Dante, definitely himself by means of metaphor, is capable of carrying the metaphor to a metamorphosis lived from within. Here he is, for example, on the last terrace of the Purgatorio, delayed with Virgil and Statius by the nocturnal law of the mountain:

Quali si stanno ruminando manse
le capre . . .
guardate dal pastor . . .
e quale il mandrian che fori alberga,
lungo il peculio suo queto pernotta . . .
tal eravam noi tutti e tre allotta
io come capra, ed ei come pastori . . .
sì ruminando e sì mirando in quelle [stelle]
mi prese il sonno. . . .

(as goats tamely ruminate . . .

as the shepherd watches over them . . .
and as the herdsman sleeps outdoors
beside his herd quietly throughout the night
so were all three of us, I like the goat
and they like shepherds, so ruminating,
and so looking at the stars sleep overcame us.)

The focus is on a sort of sublime visionary animality.

The reality upon which Dante's versatility and openness operate is experienced as history, in time, even when it is eternal and recurrent; when it descends toward determinate individual beings it is so much the more complete. Geographic reality, for example, is sampled with such fullness and freshness as to transform the *Comedy* into a sort of Golden Album of Italian scenes unmatched until Guicciardini's *History,* the work of another realist. The roar of the waterfall at San Benedetto delle Alpe and the rustling of the pine forest at Classe were obviously familiar to Dante's ears, but the vividness of description, even of places which were so much more remote, as far as the reefs of Noli or even the dikes of Flanders, is such that one is inclined to accept Bassermann's suspicion that these descriptions represent personal recollections of a man who had really been to these places. It is true that Dante's general utilization of experience does not permit us in principle to distinguish between direct, indirect, or even bookish knowledge: thus, a dictionary can be for him a mine of discoveries and the greatest one of his day, the *Magnae Derivationes* of Ugoccione da Pisa, serves the same heuristic purpose as does the dictionary of Tommaseo-Bellini for Gabriele D'Annunzio.

The lack of distinction between experience and culture has its most striking manifestation in the temporal levelling of the poet's historical personages, all of whom are summoned up as contemporaries in the poet's consciousness, before which is enacted "the state of the souls after death" — to use Dante's own words from the Epistle to Dan Grande — without temporal gradation or perspective. Even within the framework of the medieval mind, it is strikingly daring: to make a contemporary, even one who has become notorious in

local gossip, the equal of a hero of antiquity, celebrated
for his glory throughout the centuries, is to blend history
and fiction, the biblical or mythological with the merely
literary of whatever cultural level ("vidi Paris, Tristano").
It is, moreover, to fuse the symbolic with the real.

Generally speaking, what counts with these
personages is not their historic existence but rather that
which joins them together, the exemplary quality in
which catharsis is achieved. Cacciaguida says it clearly,
even if he portrays fame in a manner that is fitting only
in the highest part of Paradise.

> Però ti son mostrate in queste rote
> nel monte e nella valle dolorosa
> pur l'anime che son di fama note
> ché l'animo di quel ch' ode, non posa
> né ferma fede per essemplo ch'aia
> la sua radice incognita e nascosa.
> Né per altro argomento che non paia.

> (So in these wheels and on the mountain.
> (and in the woeful valley,
> souls that are known to fame have been
> shown to you, for the mind of him who hears
> will not pause or fix its faith for an example
> that has its roots unknown or hidden,
> nor for other evidence that is not apparent.)

This situation corresponds to the dual aspect of
the protagonist, a consequence of the realistic impos-
sibility of portraying "Man" in general. The name that
Dante must pronounce in the Purgatorio, his own, "che
di necessità qui si registra," recalls a previous instance,
that of the *Roman de la Rose*, where the character who
says "I" was the name Guillaume (that is, de Lorris, even
if it occurs in the part written by Jean de Meung). In the
Fiore, the author of that missing link (and it is *that*, even
for those who question its authenticity), the name of Ser
Durante is substituted for that of Guillaume. In another
passage, from the *Tesoretto*, not only does the protagonist
call himself Brunetto, but he also grafts both vision and
doctrine into an historic context so that his fictive
teachers can be recruited both from among the fathers of
ancient knowledge and from edifying personifications.

These crude and generic rough sketches are surpassed by Dante, thanks — above all — to the creation of a worthy deuteragonist: Beatrice. The human being who occasions, by love and by death, his supreme spiritual experience assumes a dual role comparable to that of the protagonist. Around Beatrice are scattered a small entourage of people who are at least nominally historical and take the place of (or, in one case, are superimposed upon) the allegorical constellation of companions in the *Roman de la Rose* and in the *Fiore*. By an ironic transfer, it is to the *Fiore* that we owe the kind of taste displayed in the naming of the guard of demons in the Malebolge. Then too, the catalogue of spirits in the other world, at first set forth in a tiresome, abstract and thoroughly traditional manner, come to life with a precision that reaches its peak in Francesca, and the otherworld is gradually filled with its great population. The hybridism of that population comes to perfect maturation with the encounter of Mastro Adamo with Simon the Greek, which represents the collision of the chronicle of everyday life with culture, and a multivalent culture at that, inasmuch as the counterfeiter is stretched out between the figure of Virgil and the biblical wife of Potiphar, a kind of eschatological levelling of humanity, the presupposition of which is that the past has no objective reality.

The mingling of ancient togas with people of negligible pedigree is truly antitragic, which is to say, comic. This is another manifestation of Dante's reaction with respect to his own culture; the historic levelling is an extension of caricature of the type we have called the "burlesque-realistic." It is not by chance that it reaches its extreme development in the dispute between Simon and Mastro Adamo, which transfers to the otherworld the *tenzone* between Forese Donati and Dante. Virgil condemns the base desire, the "bassa voglia" of wanting to overhear disputes such as might be represented in the poetry of Dante's Sienese friends or his correspondents, such as Cecco Angiolieri and Meuccio Tolomei, where the pure state of insult-trading between contemporary

stereotyped characters is unredeemed by the vast polytonal structure of a poem such as Dante's. Dante
approaches this complete acknowledgment of the comic
state only toward the end of his journey down into the
great funnel.

It is no accident that the *Comedy* is named for
the first time just before the descent into the Malebolge:
only in the *bolgia* of the soothsayers does Virgil mention
"l'alta *sua* tragedia," *his* high tragedy, obviously because,
at an interval of only a few verses, after the division into
a new canto, Dante cites his "commedia" in opposition.
And it is just beyond the end of the Malebolge, scene of
the climactic dispute between the two counterfeiters, that
Dante invokes his harsh and clucking rhymes, "le rime
aspre e chiocce." And the comic *cantica* closes, in a style
that is *aspro* and *chioccio*, with almost regal horrors and
misfortunes, the cannibalism of which the archbishop
Ruggieri is a victim, along with that of Brutus and his
companions. It is a true anti-tragedy, an *Aeneid* or a
Thebiades somewhat like the originals and yet somewhat
inverted.

Dante's synthesis, a competitor of the *Aeneid* (of
the *Thebiades* or the *Pharsalia*) and of the *Metamorphoses*,
surpassing by far the *Roman de la Rose* and the *Tesoretto*,
not to mention the whole tribe of poets of the grotesque,
and imitating even the Bible, is an unheard-of novelty,
and this was Dante's intention, according to his recurrent
topos: the decision "di dicer di lei quello che mai fue
detto d'alcuno" — *to say of her that which has never
been said of any other." The decision was announced at
the end of the *Vita Nuova* as a proclamation of both
formal and material novelty in the double *sestine*, in the
De Vulgari Eloquentia and in the *De Monarchia* as well.

Dante arrived at the root of this novelty quite
gradually. The *De Vulgari* asserted that "this same
tragedy" (that is, the genre to which the Aeneid and the
highest lyrics belong, according to the medieval
definition) "is resplendent through the admixture of
sweet and harsh rhymes." Is it an accident that the
treatise breaks off precisely here? — the treatise in which,

according to scholastic metaphysics, the ideal which is pursued represents the simplest and most perfect reality of the series, so that the vernacular tongue is governed by the illustrious vernacular as number by unity, color by whiteness, being by God. And this will continue to be the attitude of Dante, except that it becomes completely reversed. That extraordinary mixture of all themes, all tones and all styles, that *summa* and *compendium* of all traditions that is the masterpiece of Dante, by a stroke of genius is named for its lowest level, *Commedia*, almost as a sign of the limits of its maximum dilation.

To be named according to the lowest denomination is a declaration of liberty. The linguistic pluralism of the poem is not always aimed at expressivity in its most extreme moments of precious refinement and of the grotesque, between Alain de Lille and Rustico Filippi, but it contains expressivity as its limit. The search for extremes is relatively easy and banal; it is much more difficult to give individuality to the mean between these extremes, a mean which is nevertheless very far from the melodic quality of Petrarch's medial tone. We should rather speak of a "recitative," of a nearly prose-like quality, such as we find in the Purgatorio, almost at the center of the work, in a conversation which has about it the quality of Monteverdi. It is the conversation between Trajan and the widow:

> . . . "or aspetta
> tanto ch' i 'torni." E quella: "Segnor mio,"
> come persona in cui dolor s'affretta,
> "se tu non torni?" Ed ei: "chi fia dov'io,
> la ti farà" . . . .

This enchanting *grisaille* is activated rhythmically thanks to the admirable asymmetry between the measure of the discourse and the measure of the verse.

The "comic" novelty of Dante is also apparent in this flexibility of the relationship between prosody and syntax and is therefore bound up with the inventiveness of his meter. Two excellent philologists, Casini and Rájna, correctly recognized its antecedents in popular, or at least "humilis" culture, one of them attributing the metric linking to the sapphic strophe of the enumerative *serventese* (such as may have been, according to this suggestive hypothesis, the now lost *serventese* of Dante on the most beautiful women of Florence); the other philologist, Rájna, placing emphasis on that series of sonnets in which the sonnet, a genre of style which the *De Vulgari* puts between low and medium, becomes a true strophe, the fleeting *terzine* of which suggest a continuous texture. Of this series by far the most important is the *Fiore*, which once more turns up in our discussion. Rájna is precisely the champion of the *Fiore*'s authenticity as one of Dante's works, and he insists on its importance as Dante's "comic" apprenticeship. There is of course something very functional in the comic style, since in it is reflected the embodiment of the author's intention, an author who, if we think not only of *De Monarchia* but also of the cantos of the terrestrial paradise, is not an ascetic but is rather secular and worldly.

In the supreme moments of Dante's comic style, we can read all of the phases through which he has passed, in a state of preservation, like a fly in amber. But at this point, we must ask a final question. If Dante the stylist is in perpetual movement, does Dante the man of culture represent something that is fixed and stable?

What is true of the other thinkers of the *dolce stil nuovo* is especially true of Dante: they are not theorists unilaterally dedicated to a single thesis or system but are rather avid readers of philosophy who discover in their texts, with considerable eclecticism, reservoirs of themes and linguistic "finds" — they treat texts much as contemporary poets treat the products of existentialism, of phenomenology, or of psychoanalysis. If we grant them versatility as artists we must also grant them a flair for the experimental in their philosophy. What is ultimately the difference between the *De Vulgari Eloquentia*'s assertion of the greater nobility of the vernacular and the *Convivio*'s assertion of the greater nobility of Latin, when we consider how short a period of time elapsed between the writing of each? — or the difference between the invariability or the variability of Hebrew from the *De*

Vulgari Eloquentia to the Paradiso? Or, again, what is the significance of the *palinode* on the lunar spots or of the theory of the emergence of the land from one work to another? The contradictions reveal a preponderance of phonic or rhythmic values over significance, which seems to give a formal aspect even to what are apparently intellectual data. Dante himself admits it in the letter to Can Grande (whose authenticity has been incorrectly called into doubt for obvious reasons), when he states that the fiction of the *Comedy* is directed *"non ad speculandum, sed ad opus."* These words are written by the same hand that in the *De Monarchia*, while paying due respect to the speculative intellect and to the absolute precedence of the philosopher, as Plato would have it, nevertheless understood the two-fold task of the practical reason: *"agere atque facere,"* the spheres of political reality (*agibilia*) and of expressive reality (*factibilia*). But in the *Comedy*, a key passage for the understanding of Dante is the eulogy of Solomon, placed, not by coincidence, in the mouth of St. Thomas —

A veder tanto non surse il secondo

(No other rose to such heights of vision),

Aquinas had said of him. And when Dante is stunned by these words, St. Thomas explains that "no other King" is implied. Who, after all, went beyond Solomon? Some professional philosopher, perhaps? No. Only Adam and Christ. And therefore Solomon

> . . . chiese senno
> acciò che re sufficente fosse;
> non per sapere il numero in che enno
> li motor di qua su, osse necesse
> con contingente mai necesse fenno;
> non si est dare primum motum esse
> o se del mezzo cerchio far si puote
> triangol sì ch'un retto non avesse.

> (. . . asked for understanding
> so that he might be a worthy king;
> not to know the number of movers that there are
> here in heaven, nor if a necessary and a contingent
> ever yielded a necessary proposition,
> nor if there is a primum mobile

nor if one can inscribe a triangle
in a semi-circle such that it will not contain a right angle.)

The vision of the geometer, the dialectician, the metaphysician, the theologian, the fruits of which are displayed, even ostentatiously, in this third *cantica*, are here parodied in wisdom's own language and tone, and the parody is attributed, no less, to the greatest philosopher of the time. Here knowledge passes its limit, as did comic poetry. Dante had listened to the argument between Simon and Mastro Adamo, the extreme episode in that style, and then he had Virgil rebuke him for the "bassa voglia." Here the theorems of the knowledge which fills the whole of the poem are scaled down and limited with respect to a higher wisdom. Dante is as inclusive in the realm of theory as he is in the realm of poetic practice.

It is not only the sovereignty of his poetry but also the inclusive character of his culture, even in his speculative presuppositions and in his language so different from all others, particularly our own, that assures the survival of Dante in cultural contexts that change more and more radically. But "survival" is an inadequate term. The authentic impression of a modern man, meeting Dante, is not of an encounter with a tenacious or well-preserved survivor, but of having reached someone who has arrived at the vantage-point before him.

DANTE, HEGEL, AND THE MARIAN INSPIRATION OF THE *COMMEDIA*

First published in Dante Studies, *XCV, 1977.*

Through his influence on the criticism of Francesco De Sanctis, the German Romantic philosopher Hegel made a major contribution to what may not improperly be called the modern cult of Dante in Italy.

It was De Sanctis, more than anyone else, who taught Italians to see in Dante the towering greatness which the best critics of German and England and America had already seen, and it was Hegel who directed De Sanctis's vision. As Professor Daisy Fornacca Kouzel has ably shown,[1] despite occasional disavowals, the great Italian critic "in most respects remained a thorough Hegelian to the end." In all his criticism, especially in the *Storia della letteratura italiana,* De Sanctis's treatment of Dante is, as Professor Kouzel says. "unquestionably Hegelian," in substance and terminology.

De Sanctis read with care Hegel's pages on Dante in the *Philosophy of Fine Art* (or *Aesthetics,* as they are called in the more recent translations).[2] And if we do the same, taking those pages in the context of Hegel's wide-ranging discussion of medieval art, we cannot fail to see how directly his penetrating appreciation of the *Divine Comedy* links him to the theme of this discussion. The same Mary, Virgin Mother of God, whose divine love joined with the human love of Beatrice leads Dante out of his *selva oscura,* apparently also gave Hegel his profoundest philosophical insight into the aesthetic consciousness of medieval Christendom: an "aesthetic consciousness" which was — as Bernard Bosanquet characterizes it in his *History of Aesthetics* — "the most continuous and creative the world has ever seen."[3]

1.

According to Bosanquet (writing, like De Sanctis, under direct Hegelian influence), the revival of ancient aesthetic theory in the early Italian Renaissance threw

into temporary eclipse the Christian-national aesthetic
consciousness that had shaped the masterworks of
medieval art. In Italy, that "great art-age of the world," as
Bosanquet calls it, which produced the weightless figures
of the Ravennese mosaics, the massively gracious Marian
churches and cathedrals, the love-suffused paintings of
Franciscan inspiration, and the poetry of Dante, began
indeed "to draw to its close in Raphael, although by
special causes it was prolonged in other countries so as
just to cover our Shakespearean drama." It had not been
a critical age. But the same could be said of the age of
Greek art that gave us Homer and Sophocles and
everything in between. The Greeks of that time had been
too busy *making* works of art to criticize or theorize about
them. Drawing a parallel, Bosanquet does not hesitate to
say of the Middle Ages: "A self-criticizing theory could no
more be expected of such an age, in spite of its not small
intellectual equipment, than of Athens before the time of
Socrates."[4]

As the recently revived Ciceronian and Aristotelian spirit of criticism worked its way up from Italy
through the Northern countries, it found itself at a loss,
initially, before the sheer bulk and novelty of the
medieval legacy of a thousand formative years. "The
architecture, painting, language, and literature of
France, Italy, and England alone," Bosanquet reminds
us, "form a material which could not be organized by
reflection in one or two generations."[5]

The recently-revived classical writings themselves
proved to be a much more amenable subject-matter for a
recently-revived classicizing criticism. The classical forms,
such criticism hastened to conclude, are enough for art,
and any content that claims to be or proves to be too
much for such forms ought therefore to be rejected as
unartistic in its very essence.

That remained for several centuries the unchal-
lenged criterion of humanistic criticism. Eventually, the
force of the present made itself felt, and a great battle of
the books occurred. Can nothing be said, it was asked in
the name of reason, for the living and breathing moderns

as against the ancients? The rationalizing moderns gradually prevailed, and criteria of rationality first supplemented and eventually undermined and totally discredited humanistic devotion to classical forms in aesthetic criticism. In the process, the legacy of the Middle Ages was even more darkly eclipsed. In fact, not until the energies of the classicizing or rationalizing anti-medievalists began to peter out in the eighteenth century was it possible for a few pioneering spirits, imbued with a living sense of history, to point out convincingly a scandalously obvious truth: namely, that despite the prevailing standards, Dante and Shakespeare unmistakably towered over the writers of the so-called Renaissance and Age of Reason at least as high as Homer and the great lyric and dramatic poets of Greece's golden age tower over the writers of the post-Socratic sophisticated age of criticism.

Irrepressible appreciation of the greatness of Dante and Shakespeare marked the start of an era we have long since come to characterize as Romantic. The notion of an essentially European and Christian *romantic* art, as distinct from the *symbolic* art of the oriental peoples, as well as from the *classical* art of the ancient Greeks and Romans, gradually shaped itself. And historically-minded critics began to use it for the precise purpose of "organizing by reflection" the great medieval national artistic legacies of France, Italy, England, and Spain, and eventually Germany as well, which had proved too much for rationalistic and humanistic criticism to digest. The content of those legacies, medievalizing critics eventually began to allege, was indeed too much for the forms of classical art. Their Christian and national vitality could express itself fully, some few presumed to say, only in forms that forced aesthetic consciousness, spiritually, beyond itself to heights where artistic activity in fact transcends itself as art.

How this thoroughly Hegelian view Bosanquet gives us of the origins of Romantic aesthetics links up with modern critical appreciation of Dante as the medieval Christian poet *par excellence* is obvious. In the

Vita Nuova, in the letter to Can Grande, and in the *Commedia* itself, Dante tells us in a variety of ways that he has had an aesthetic experience so transcendent that no other poet who might conceivably have experienced it — not Homer, not Virgil — had ever dared to make it his theme. For its adequate expression, the forms of classical perfection and the powers of Apollonian and Dionysian inspiration taken together simply could not suffice. He has been moved to write, says Dante, not merely to give ideal embodiment to a vision of perfect beauty in the Greek fashion, nor even to raise a worshipful hymn of praise to unutterable divinity, in the Hebraic or oriental fashion; his claim is that he has been singled out providentially to provide nothing less than a new Holy Writ for mankind: a sacred poem (*poema sacro*) which by God's grace will have in its beauty a truly sacramental power "to remove those living in this life from a state of misery, and to bring them to a state of happiness."[6]

A sudden, almost Pentacostal gift of words, dictated by love in his heart, has made him presume, Dante says, not only to vie with Homer and Virgil as an epic poet but even and quite literally to "write like God"[7] for mankind's spiritual salvation. Where art fails, the Word of divine love supplies the deficiency — that very Word which was made flesh in the womb of Mary so that He might later, for mankind's salvation in love, be crucified on the wood of the Cross.

At the close of the *Commedia,* where he tells us he has seen the oneness of the triune, three-personed God (each person of Whom is the whole trinity in Himself), with man's effigy (the manhood of Christ crucified) at its center, Dante pushes art to its absolute limits, saying that for such an experience his own wings could in no way suffice except that, in the very moment of their failure, his "mind was smitten by a sudden flash that gave it what it willed" (". . . la mia mente fu percossa/da un folgore in che sua voglia venne," *Par.* XXXIII, 140-141).[8]

But sight is one thing and art another. Passing beyond art's limits, but remaining somehow all the more an artist, Dante concludes with must be the consummate expression of Romantic self-transcendence in the highest reaches of art:

> A l'alta fantasia qui mancò possa;
> ma già volgea il mio disio e 'l *velle*,
> sì come rota ch'igualmente è mossa,
> l'amor che move il sole e l'altre stelle.
>
> (*Par.* XXXIII, 142-145)

The love that moves the stars is the same love that dictates the *Commedia* to Dante. He is halfway through life's journey, astray in a *selva oscura*, when he first becomes aware of its directive presence. It comes to him through a long chain of command, but it comes decisively, with gracious force enough to compel him upon "another journey" ("un altro viaggio") that will make him, upon his return, "write like God." As links in that chain of compelling grace, Dante has, he specifies, the intercession of Virgil for the perfection of his poetic art, of Beatrice for purification of his carnal intellect, of Lucy for the strengthening of his eyes to sustain the otherwise overwhelming light of the divine vision, and of Mary, finally, to open up his heart to that same divine love that will fill him with grace, even as she was filled with grace when the Word was made flesh in her womb.

2.

Like the great churches of "notre dame" raised throughout Christendom in the Middle Ages, the *Commedia* is unmistakably a work of art of Marian inspiration. Roman Catholic piety has in recent years catalogued the textual evidences, most ably perhaps in Pierina Valmacco's tenderly beautiful labor of love, *La Madonne nella Divina Commedia.*[9] But to grasp the high aesthetic significance of that inspiration, with insight sustained by a commanding philosophic power, we have only to turn, as Francesco De Sanctis and Bernard Bosanquet turned so profitably, to the pages of Hegel's *Aesthetics*, where he defines the characteristic principle of *romantic* art, as distinct from *classical* and *symbolic* art.[10]

What Hegel says there of the Christian romantic or Marian inspiration of the *Commedia* and of medieval art in general is not some isolated contribution to the nineteenth-century cult of the Middle Ages. On the contrary, it is part of a rounded aesthetics that says as much for the classical art of the Greeks with their ideal of perfect beauty and for the symbolic art of the oriental peoples with their sense of the disquieting sublimity of divine power, as for the romantic art of the Europeans with its Christian emphasis on love.

Beauty, power, and love: in terms of these three principles, Hegel distinguishes not only the classical, symbolic, and romantic types of art but also the diverse concepts of divinity of the people who have characteristically produced those types of art. The Greek nation, he writes, made its essential spirit

> visible for its intuition and imaginative consciousness through the representation of its gods, giving them by means of art a well-defined existence that accords with their true content. By virtue of this complete adequacy of form and content which characterizes Greek art in its essential concept . . . art becomes in Greece the highest expression for the absolute, and Greek religion is thus the religion of art itself."[11]

In the best art of a people that sees divinity most plainly in its own perfected human spirit, beauty is truth, truth is beauty — that is all they know on earth and all they need to know, But it has been quite otherwise, maintains Hegel, for the non-Greek peoples of the ancient world whose religious experience, however vague it may have been, always transcended the expressive powers of art; and it has been otherwise also for the peoples of the post-classical West, where the Hellenic heritage of artistic beauty, eudaemonistic ethics, and speculative philosophy has been orientalized, or — more precisely — Hebraicized, in the faith of Christianity.

Among the non-Greek peoples for whom God is unfathomable mystery or annihilating necessity or outpouring love, artistic expression must of necessity, says Hegel, either fall short of or transcend the perfection of the classical ideal in which intention and expression, content and form, are reciprocally adequate. Falling short of that ideal, art is and remains essentially symbolic, regardless of the level of skill attained by the artist or the medium of expression used. At its worst, it is an art of unnatural shapes, confused colors, weird sounds, and hieroglyphs, while at its best it is, as Hegel observes, awe-inspiring in its "aspirations, its disquiet, its mystery, and its sublimity."[12]

On the other hand, where art does not fall short of the classical ideal of reciprocal adequacy but transcends it, the mode of expression becomes *romantic*, which is, in the Hegelian terminology, the extreme opposite of *symbolic*. Of such art he does not hesitate to say that while it is indeed still art, it nevertheless "already points to a higher form of consciousness than art can provide." (Knox trans., p. 438) In its grandest achievements, it expressed profounder depths of spirituality than classical art has ever attempted to express and manages to express them better than the medium and manner of artistic expression would seem to allow, so that the result finally is art pushed to its limits, on the point of "transcending itself as art."

Christianity of course shares with Judaism and Mohammedanism that sublime sense of transcendent omnipotent divinity which is the inspiration of symbolic art; but while in the experience of the two other great monotheistic religions cradled in the Middle East, the one true God remains unutterable even in name (though the whole creation is deemed to be his utterance), in Christianity it is otherwise. That very God of Abraham, Isaac, and Jacob — so Christian faith holds — has been brought down out of his sublime transcendence into the world, as the Word made flesh, visibly and memorably incarnate, and therefore depictable by art as at once divine and human. In this respect, according to Hegel, the incarnation makes possible a synthesis of the classical and symbolic attitudes.

In the early Middle Ages, especially in the Eastern half of the Christianized Roman Empire, there was a powerful iconoclastic movement that very nearly deprived Christendom of representational art. Under the pressure of image-hating Neo-Platonic deists, as well as powerful minorities of Mohammedans and Jews, who were at once affluent and fervent, the Christian emperors of the East were from time to time ready to impose a total ban on "humanistic" art. As Adolf von Harnack stresses in his monumental *Lehrbuch der Dogmengeschichte*, what was ultimately at stake in the controversy was nothing less than the divinity of the incarnate Christ. "Had God not become man," said Gregory II in reply to an iconoclastic imperial edict of the eighth century, "we would not portray him in human form."[13] In strict fidelity to that principle, a fully rounded aesthetic consciousness, creative in sculpture, painting, and poetry, as well as in architecture and music, was secured an unchallengeable place in Western medieval Christendom.

In his *Aesthetics*, Hegel dwells on the subject. With regard to the truth of Christian faith, there is a sense — he says — in which "art, taken purely as art, is superfluous."[14] The high Divinity Itself, as spirit, is

> not an immediate topic for art. Its supreme actual reconciliation within itself can only be a reconciliation and satisfaction in the spiritual as such, and this in its purely ideal element is not susceptible of expression in art, since absolute truth is on a higher level than the appearance of beauty which cannot be detached from the soil of the sensuous and apparent. (Knox, p.539)

Having made that concession to the logic of the iconoclasts, Hegel hastens to add:

> On the other hand, the religious material [of the redemptive history of Christ] contains in itself at the same time a factor whereby it is not only made accessible to art but does in a certain respect actually *need* art.

The appearance of God in time, in historical particularity, needs artistic representation to make it present to the contemplative consciousness of later times. Here art provides

> the special presence of an actual individual shape, a concrete picture too of the external features of the events in which Christ's birth, life and sufferings, death, resurrection, and Ascension to the right hand of God are displayed, so that, in general, the actual appearance of God, which has passed away, is repeated and perpetually renewed in art alone. (Knox, p. 535)

God's appearance on earth is, of course, for Christendom an appearance of love. In the course of history, man has known many kinds of love ranging from carnal *eros* at the bottom of the Platonic *scala amoris* to the purity of *eros philosophicos* at its top and soaring far beyond that into the *agape* of the Mosaic commandment to "love the Lord thy God with all thy heart, and with all thy soul, and with all thy might." The true essence of genuine love, Hegel writes, "consists in giving up the consciousness of oneself, forgetting oneself in another self, yet, in this surrender and oblivion, having and possessing oneself alone." (Knox, pp. 539-540) What is manifest in the love-birth and love-death of Christ, he explains, "is on the one hand God himself, in his invisible essence, and, on the other, mankind which is to be redeemed, and thus what then comes into appearance in Christ is less the absorption of one person in another limited person than the idea of love in its universality." (Knox, p. 541)

For art, the great moments of the Christian drama are the Annunciation, where the burning Seraph aflame with love says to Mary, "Hail, full of grace"; the moments of the babe in the manger, and the infant in his mother's arms; the earthly ministry among friends and enemies; and finally the rending human passion (*Zerrissenheit*) of the crucifixion and descent from the Cross in death which is made humanly bearable only by the presence of Mary, whose grief is suffused throughout with a sense of absolute reconciliation in the peace of divine love which passes all understanding.

Here one must pause for a moment to stress that, in his major writings and lectures on religion — which are voluminous — Hegel develops a Christology, a theology, and an ecclesiology with little reference to art or to the Virgin Mary. Indeed, as a philosophizing Lutheran, he can hardly resist saying at one point that, however great it may have been in the Middle Ages, Christianity's religious need for art can be and has in fact been overcome through the Protestant Reformation.

For when the Spirit brings itself into consciousness of itself in its own element, separated from the whole natural grounding which feeling supplies, it is only spiritual mediation, free from such grounding, that can be regarded as the free route to truth; and so, Protestantism, in contrast with the mariolatry in art and faith, the Holy Spirit and the inner mediation of the Spirit has become the higher truth.[15]

Still, when his concern is not Christology, theology, or ecclesiology, but the aesthetic consciousness of Christendom, Hegel does not hesitate to bring the incarnation of divine love, through Mary, into focus, as the highest conceivable inspiration that art has ever had. The pages on Mary in the *Aesthetics* in fact provide the key to his entire discussion of romantic art and read in retrospect like a literary as well as a philosophical explication of the meaning of St. Bernard's prayer to Mary in the concluding canto of the Paradiso. In Hegel's words:

Mary's love for the Christ child, the love of the one mother who has borne the Saviour of the world in her arms, is the most beautiful subject to which Christian art has risen . . . . Thus, religious love in its fullest and most intimate human form, we contemplate not in the suffering and risen Christ or in his lingering among his friends but in the person of Mary with her womanly feeling. Mary's whole heart and being is human love for the child that she calls her own, and at the same time adoration, worship, and love of God with whom she feels herself at one. She is humble in God's sight and yet has an infinite sense of being the one woman who is blessed above all other virgins. She is not subsistent on her own account, but is perfect only in her child, in God, but in him she is satisfied and blessed, whether at the manger or as the Queen of heaven, without passion or longing, without any further need, without aim other than to have and to hold what she has. In its religious subject matter the portrayal of this love has a wide series of events . . . which presents the peace and full satisfaction of love.[16]

That love-filled peace is, however, followed by the deepest suffering. "Mary sees Christ carry his cross," writes Hegel, "she sees him suffer and die on the cross, taken down from the cross and buried, and no grief of others is so profound as hers." (Knox, p. 825) Still, the real burden of her suffering is not the "unyieldingness of grief or of loss only, nor the weight of a necessary imposition, nor complaint about the injustice of fate." (Knox, p. 825) And here, focusing with precision on the characteristic difference, with respect to content, between classical and romantic art, Hegel introduces a provocative comparison with Homer's Niobe, who has also "lost all her children." The beauty of Niobe's characteristic grief confronts us, he observes,

> in pure sublimity and unimpaired beauty. What is kept here is the aspect of her existence as an unfortunate woman, the beauty that has become her nature and makes up the whole of her existence in reality; her actual individuality remains what it is in her beauty. But her inner life, her heart, has lost the whole burden of its love and its soul; her individuality and beauty can only turn into stone. Mary's grief is of a totally different kind. She is emotional, she feels the thrust of the dagger into the center of her soul, her heart breaks, but she does not turn into stone. She did not only *have* love; on the contrary, her whole inner life *is* love, the free concrete spiritual depth of feeling which preserves the absolute essence of what she has lost, and even in the loss of the loved one she ever retains the peace of love. Her heart breaks; but the very substance and burden of her heart and mind which shines through her soul's suffering with a vividness never to be lost is something infinitely higher. This is the living beauty of *soul* in contrast to the abstract *substance* which, when its ideal existence in the body perishes, remains imperishable, but in stone .(Knox, p. 826)

In Hegel's view, it was the challenge of depicting divine love in Mary that raised modern painting to heights surpassing by far anything attempted by the Romans or Greeks, or the Indians, Chinese, or Egyptians before them. And the links between Giotto and Dante on this theme are greatly illuminated by the Hegelian insights. "In antiquity," he writes, "many excellent portraits may have been painted but neither the classical treatment of natural objects nor its vision of human or divine affairs was of such a kind as to make possible in painting the expression of such depths of spirituality as was presented in Christian painting." (Knox, p. 801) In Mary full of grace, the depth of Christian feeling attains an expression of absolute spiritual beauty, of the ideal, human identification of Man with God, with the spirit and with truth: a pure forgetfulness and complete self-surrender which still in this forgetfulness is from the beginning one with that into which it is merged and now with blissful satisfaction has a sense of this oneness. . . . [Only[in the form of feeling is the Spirit made prehensible by art, and the feeling of the unity between the individual and God is present in the most original, real, and living way only in the Madonna's maternal love. This love must enter art necessarily if, in the portrayal of this sphere, the ideal, the affirmative satisfied reconciliation is not to be lacking. There was therefore a time when the maternal love of the Blessed Virgin belonged in general to the highest and holiest and was worshipped and represented as this supreme fact. (Knox, p. 542)

All that Christian architecture built and all that Christian painting delineated, with the attendant embellishments of sculpture and music, is gathered up for consummate epic, lyric, and even dramatic representation in the total world of the *Commedia*, which is for Hegel "the most beautiful and richest work in this sphere, the artistic epic proper of the Christian Catholic Middle Ages, its greatest poem with the greatest material content." Contrasting Dante with Homer, Hegel notes that whereas the people of the *Iliad* and *Odyssey* "have been made permanent in *our* memories by the muse, the characters of Dante have produced their situations for *themselves*, as individuals, and are eternal in themselves, not in our ideas. The immortality created by the poet's *mnemòsyne* counts here objectively as the very judgment of God. . . . There are glimpses of antiquity in the world of the Catholic poet, but antiquity is only a guiding star and a comparison of human wisdom and culture, for, when it is a matter of doctrine and dogma, it is only the scholasticism of Christian theology and love which speaks."[17]

3.

One needs to stress here that the Marian love of Dante's poem, like its theology, is not a creature of Dante's poetic imagination. It is not by studying Dante that we can best comprehend its substantiality. Our own Henry Adams (who in his *Mont Saint Michel and Chartres* sets the Italian text of Dante's great prayer to Mary beside Petrarch's and reminds us that Chaucer translated Dante's in the "Second Nonnes Tale") notes how "the Virgin filled so enormous a space in the life and thought of the time that one stands now helpless before the mass of testimony to her direct action and constant presence in every moment and form. . . ."[18]

After suggesting that there was "no special reason why" the twelfth and thirteenth centuries "should have so passionately flung themselves," as they did, "at the feet of the Woman rather than of the Man," Adams nevertheless offers this thoroughly Dantesque and we might also say Hegelian explanation:

> Men were, after all, not wholly inconsequent; their attachment to Mary rested on an instinct of self-preservation. They knew their own peril. If there is to be a future life, Mary was their only hope. She alone represented Love. The Trinity were, or was, One, and could by the nature of its essence, administer Justice alone. Only childlike illusion could expect a personal favor . . . turn the dogma as one would, to this it must logically come. Call the three Godheads by what names one liked, still they must remain One; must administer one justice; must admit only one law. In that law, no human weakness or error could exist; by its very essence it was infinite, eternal, immutable. There was no crack and no cranny in the system through which human frailty could hope for escape. One was forced from corner to corner by a remorseless logic until one fell helpless at Mary's feet. . . . Without Mary, man had no hope except in atheism, and for atheism the world was not yet ready. Hemmed back on that side, men rushed like sheep to escape the butcher, and were driven to Mary; only too happy in finding protection and hope in a being who could understand the language they talked, and the excuses they had to offer.[19]

Readers of Adams no doubt have visited Rock Creek Cemetery in Washington D.C, where "Grief" (the woman's figure St. Gaudens made for Henry Adams as a memorial for Adams' wife) keeps an ageless vigil. And if they are readers of Dante as well, they surely have seen at once what the difference is between the help of Mary and the hope of atheism as opposed here by Adams. Adams cites Shakespeare's line from *1 Henry IV* — "Christ's mother helps, else I were too weak!" — spoken by the Maid of Orleans, and Gaunt's allusion to "the world's ransom, Blessed Mary's son"[20] as the last traces of genuine medieval Catholicism in English art, before the start of the modern era that is turned upon itself not by love but by the power of a whirring mechanical dynamo. Only in those verses is there a significant link through Marian inspiration between Shakespeare and Dante; and yet there is everywhere in the great English dramatist an overwhelming tragic sense of the loss of that help without which, as Hegel says, art cannot portray the reconciliation of the human in the divine made possible by the *Liebestod* of the Cross.

In Dante's native Florence, no less than in Henry Adams' Chartres, the power of Mary was an omnipresent artistic reality. The city's greatest churches were dedicated to her, and masterworks of Marian inspiration by Cimabue, Duccio, and Giotto graced their walls. What architecture, sculpture, and painting can do in granite, marble, bronze, and pigments, Dante attempts in his poem; and his words, where their appeal is directly to the pictorial imagination, have inspired many artists since to picture for the sensual eye the visions of his mind's eye.

In the Inferno, Dante avoids explicit mention of Mary or her Son by name. As Virgil reports it in the second canto, when Beatrice came to him in hell, to enlist his help, she freely named herself and Lucy as links in the chain of grace that was being extended to Dante. But of Mary's intercession at the top end of the chain, she speaks in words suitable for a pagan's ear:

> Donna è gentil nel ciel che si compiange
> di questo 'mpedimento ov'io ti mando,
> sì che duro giudicio là sù frange.
>
> (*Inf.* II, 94-96)

In the Purgatorio and Paradiso, however, that *donna gentil* is directly invoked as *Maria* at least twenty times and as *Vergine, Madre, Donna,* and *Regina* many times more. The structure of Purgatorio is defined through references to her virtues in the form of moral lessons. On each level of the seven-storied mountain a scene from her life is introduced as an example to those who are purging their sins: for the proud, she is humility; for the envious, she is self-denying generosity; for the wrathful, she is meekness; for the slaves of sloth, she is eagerness; for the avaricious, she is blessed poverty; for the gluttonous, she is temperance; and for the lustful, she is chastity.

Integral parts of the overall aesthetic design of the *cantica*, — always masterfully plastic — the Marian representations also trace for us what might be called "a progression of the fine arts," in an altogether Hegelian manner. The moral "exempla" are first given three-dimensional architectural and sculptural representation, which are, in the system of Hegelian aesthetic, the symbolic and classical media par excellence. Three-dimensionality gives way in stages to surface representations of painting, to musical expression with its purely temporal dimensions, and finally to poetry which, with its narrative, lyrical, and dramatic voices, can utter into being (through the non-dimensional point of focus of our aesthetic consciousness) an architecture, sculpture, painting, and music all its own. Integrating this purgatorial progression of the arts is Mary's exemplary presence, which makes it, by the end of the *cantica*, an aesthetic tour de force in her honor.[21]

What happens in the Purgatorio by virtue of Mary's presence serves also to prepare Dante and his readers for the journey of the Paradiso, where poetry will attempt to soar to heights never before approached by human art. On each level of his heavenly *scala amoris*, Dante supplies us with touchstones of high poetry built on Marian images. In the lowest and least bright of the heavenly spheres, that of the inconstant moon, Piccarda — who failed to keep her religious vows — is represented as being in constant prayer to Mary, a prayer at once of penitence and grateful fulfillment. When Dante asks her whether she longs for a higher, brighter place in heaven, she replies, ". . . 'n sua volontade è nostra pace. . . . (*Par.* III, 85), which clarifies for Dante the meaning of heaven. And when she has told the tale of how, against her will, she was dragged from the convent of St. Clare and forced to resume a worldly life, Dante comments:

> Così parlommi, e poi cominciò
> "*Ave Maria*" cantando, e cantando vanio. . . .
>
> (Par. III, 121-122)

We cannot examine here every use Dante makes of Marian images as he leads us upward through the *cantica* of light into the Empyrean but before coming to focus on the distinctly Marian cantos at the end of Paradiso we should note, at least in passing, one or two instances that have a particular bearing on our theme, starting with the extraordinary image of the eleventh canto, where Mary is literally put down by comparison with another woman. That canto is Dante's sublime tribute to St. Francis; and if Mary is indeed put down there, it is of her own will — so that when she remains below at the crucifixion, our lady Poverty (that "other woman" in her Son's life) may rise with Christ on the cross to be his bride in death:

> sì che, dove Maria rimase giuso,
> ella con Cristo pianse in su la croce.
>
> (*Par.* XI, 71-72)

Prudent Solomon in Canto XIV is said to speak as unassumingly as no doubt the Angel spoke to Mary; and Dante's brave ancestor Cacciaguida in the following canto says that, responding to his mother's deep cries of labor, it was Mary who gave him birth. With Canto XXIII we come in sight of the Virgin rose of the redeemed:

> Quivi è la rosa, in che 'l verbo divino
> carne si fece. . . .
>
> (*Par.* XXIII, 73-74)

Gabriel, who calls himself angelic love ("io sono amore angelico"), addresses Mary by name as he circles around her.

> " , , , e girerommi, donna del ciel, mentre
> che seguirai tuo figlio, e farai dia
> più la spera supprema, perchè lì entre."
> Così la circulata melodia
> si sigillava, e tutti lì altri lumi
> facean sonare il nome di Maria.
>
> (*Par.* XXIII, 106-111)

In the same canto, Dante later uses the image of an infant reaching out for his mother to suggest how the redeemed reached out in love toward Mary, as they sang *Regina coeli*. And marking the heavenly place of St. Peter, Dante says in the canto's concluding lines:

Quivi triunfa, sotto l'alto Filio
di Dio e di Maria, di sua vittoria.
e con l'antico e col novo concilio,
colui che tien le chiavi di tal gloria.
(*Par.* XXIII, 136-139)

4.

In Virgil's account of the chain of command that sent him to Dante's aid at the edge of the *selva oscura*, the links upward to the will of God are all female. Beatrice comes to Virgil at Lucy's bidding and Lucy has been moved by Mary's direct intercession. In the actual ascent to Mary, for reasons of poetry and chivalric grace as well as theology, however, a male link is interspersed. In the thirty-first canto, after he has seen all the lights of the Church triumphant and the angelic choir in their heavenly places, Dante is finally led to a holy elder who replaces Beatrice as his guide. The elder's intercession is necessary, Dante is told, so that he may complete his journey perfectly — "acciò che tu assommi/perfettamente . . . il tuo cammino" (*Par.* XXXI, 94-95). Lucy will be given her due, finally, as the last named of the saints in Dante's catalog of the celestial rose. Lucy moved Mary, we are told, but it is the holy elder, dispatched by prayer and holy love, as he says, who intercedes to show Dante how he can and must strengthen his eyes to see what he has taken his *altro viaggio* to see. Assuring Dante that his intercession here suffices, the elder says:

E la regina del cielo, ond'io ardo
tanto d'amor, ne farà ogni grazia,
però ch'i' sono il suo fedel Bernardo.
(*Par.* XXXI, 100-102)

St. Bernard directs Dante's sight to the remotest circles, where heaven's Queen is enthroned and there he sees smiling

. . . una bellezza, che letizia
era ne li occhi a tutti li altri santi.

(*Par.* XXXI, 100-102)

With his eyes on Mary, Dante gives us another of a long series of protests of artistic incompetence to portray what he has seen — protests which he carries straight through to the end of the *Commedia*:

> e s'io avessi in dir tanta divizia
>   quanta ad imaginar, non ardirei
>   lo minimo tentar di sua delizia.
>   (*Par.* XXXI, 136-138)

The poet is not yet ready to fix his gaze on Mary's bright joy. To exercise and strengthen him, St. Bernard in the next canto directs Dante to visualize the celestial rose of the elect in its full-blossomed entirety. Among its petals, as along the graded tiers of a vast amphitheater, are seated, in one half, all the saints who looked forward faithfully to Christ's coming, and in the other half (where there are still some vacant places), all those who believed in Christ after he had come. Mary's place is central and on the highest tier among the forward-looking believers; and the corresponding uppermost and central place on the opposite side is John the Baptist's. In the tier just below Mary sits Eve, who opened the wound that Mary, in the fullness of time, closed and anointed ("che Maria richiuse ed unse," [*Par.* XXXII, 4]). Only after he has marked the places of all the elect on the lower tiers does Bernard redirect Dante's strengthened sight back to heaven's Queen:

> Riguarda omai ne la faccia che a Cristo
>   più si somiglia, che la sua chiarezza
>   sola ti può disporre a veder Cristo.
>   (*Par.* XXXII, 86-87)

Dante then paints us a series of pictures of Mary's angel Gabriel that do for the inner eye in a flash all that the brush and pigments of the ablest painters of the subject do for our outer sight. A single *terzina* gives us this magnificent Annunciation:

> e quello amor che primo lì discese,
>   cantando "*Ave Maria, gratia plena*,"
>   dinanzi a lei le sue ali distese.
>   (*Par.* XXXII, 94-96)

Questioning Bernard about the angel, Dante gives us a sense of the painter's burden — which Hegel profoundly explores in his *Aesthetics* — in attempting to depict the spirituality of divine love in human features:

> qual è quell'angel, che con tanto gioco
> guarda ne li occhi la nostra regina,
> innamorato sì che par di fuoco?
> (*Par.* XXXII, 103-105)

Bernard answers with still another brief but precisely-pictured Annunciation:

> elli è quelli che portò la palma
> giuso a Maria, quando 'l Figliuol di Dio
> carcar si volse de la nostra salma.
> (*Par.* XXII, 112-113)

Yet, even Gabriel, it appears, has been a "forced" distraction, to further strengthen the poet's sight. Bernard now invites Dante to focus on the uppermost tier of the rose where, flanking Mary left and right, the "great patricians of this most just and pious empire" sit. (*Par.* XXXII, 116-118)l Identifying Adam on the left and Peter on the right, Bernard says:

> Quei due che seggon la sù più felici
> per esser propinquissimi ad Augusta,
> son d'esta rosa quasi due radici.
> (*Par.* XXXII, 118-120)

Further left and right, Moses and John are paired, and then Anna and Lucy, who now gets her poetic due as the saintly intercessor who moved Beatrice ("che mosse la tua donna" [*Par.* XXXII, 137]) when Dante seemed bent upon his own destruction.

Here the guided tour of heaven must stop. It is time, Bernard says, to turn our eyes to the Primal Love ("al primo amore"). And for that, he warns, if you are not to fail while thinking you have succeeded you must first gain grace, by prayer, from her who has the means to help you ("da quella che può aiutarti"). Mary's faithful Bernard will utter the holy prayer ("questa santa orazione"), but Dante will follow it with his love, so that his heart will be inseparably fused with every word of it.

Bernard's prayer to the Mother of God fills with Marian grace the first thirteen *terzine* or thirty-nine verses (13 x 3) of the thirty-third and concluding canto of the third *cantica* of the *Commedia*. In his *Mont Saint Michel and Chartres*, where he supplies parallel English translations for all other texts cited in ancient or modern foreign languages, Henry Adams quotes most of this great prayer only in Italian, noting lightly that even the heavenly power of Mary celebrated there — a power that sufficed to raise the greatest cathedrals of Europe — has its obvious limits: for not the "whole Trinity, with the Virgin to aid," could possibly have power enough, he concludes, to pardon the fool who would attempt a translation."[22]

The Bernadian prayer defies translation as poetry precisely because Dante compresses into it all the power that has in fact raised him, as a poet, above poetry. To comprehend the prayer's *greatness* as poetry, one must take it *literally* — which means, in the translator's art, without poetic license for the sake of rhythm or rhyme or idiomatic imagery. As T. S. Eliot expressed it in his essay "What Dante Means to Me": "No verse seems to demand greater literalness in translation than Dante's, because no poet convinces one more completely that the word he has used is the word he wanted, and that no other will do."[23] Eliot further observes that "of the very few poets of similar stature [he ranks Shakespeare, Homer, and Virgil with Dante] there is none, not even Virgil, who has been a more attentive student of the *art* of poetry, or a more scrupulous, painstaking and *conscious* practitioner of the *craft*."[24] Pressing his poetic craft to the highest reaches of perfection, Dante indeed transcends art's limits, and he is manifestly *conscious* of doing so in Bernard's prayer. Into the idea of the divine word made flesh in the womb of Mary, he there pours a wealth of speculative thought so rich that it boggles the mind. It is Plato and Aristotle (and Hegel), as well as the Gospels, St. Augustine, and St. Thomas. But it is such thought dictated by love in unquestionably *living words*.

Dante, it has been said, is unique in this: that in our contemporary world people turn to him to read his works not just as a poet on a par with Homer and Shakespeare but rather as a spiritual guide — the way he himself in his poem turns to Virgil first, then to Beatrice and St. Bernard, and finally to Mary. Here it would not be out of place to cite some unpublished words of a great teacher who in the first half of the century opened up the pages of Dante in this way, as a spiritual guide as well as poet, to literally hundreds of men and women who went on, in turn, to do the same for others through teaching and writing.

"Why do people turn to Dante?" he used to ask.

Who are those who read and admire him today — besides us: professors who have to earn their salary teaching something or students who have to subject themselves to a certain amount of serious reading to get a degree?. . . . The great clientele for Dante these days is to be found among those who have experienced life with all its deficiencies, who have been stung by this man-made life of ours with its personal and social materialism, or who are hurt by the realization that the more we know, the more obvious becomes the misery, the more sharp the agony of life. People who are discouraged with what men actually do, in other words, take refuge in Dante. People much perplexed, anguished by the situation surrounding them, look for a haven and think that they find it in Dante. Many of the recent books on Dante touch on this. . . . Why don't they turn to theologians, philosophers? Why Dante? The answer is obvious. Not being theologians or philosophers them-selves, they turn to a kindred spirit — someone who has gone through their kind of experience, and almost drowned, to use Dante's words. The theologian, the preacher, leaves them rather cold. It is the poetic element in him, of course, that attracts with its spiritual warmth. The infinitely suggestive imaginative power in his words pulls us into his life. His poem becomes ours, we pour ourselves into its divine form. That is the greatness of a work of art: its capacity to grow in meaning, to expand in significance as we bring ourselves to it. Which is to say, a poem is not made simply by the poet who writes it down, but is constantly recreated by those who read it. I could cite a dozen recent works by Dante scholars, by poets and novelists, in which you see the process at work. These people take Dante and build up out of his text a sort of ideal character that meets their needs, a character that changes and yet remains the same. . . . On his poem, in other words, has been heaped all the emotions of many generations of imaginative readers. And, as we read it today, we must not be, and cannot be blind to the fact that it has been a gospel for many people — a this-worldly gospel, for the most part. . . . We must not suppose that Dante, when we read him today, is a lifeless document, fixed just the way it was registered by Dante's pen, any more than a child of yours could remain that fertilized egg of conception in its mother's womb. No. Dante is what his readers have poured into him all these centuries.[25]

These words are from the unpublished manuscript of lectures on "The Philosophical Backgrounds of the *Divine Comedy*," delivered at Columbia University in 1954 by the eminent Dino Bigongiari, the most prominent medieval and Renaissance scholar of the twentieth century, certainly one of the greatest Dante scholars of all time. His mastery of classical and medieval culture was judged by his peers to be unmatched anywhere.

The image with which he concludes the passage just quoted — of the fertilized egg in a mother's womb — is especially appropriate for our theme, the Marian inspiration of the *Commedia*; and the living germ of its growth is to be found in the prayer of St. Bernard. First comes praise of Mary as Mother of God (*Theotókos*), expressed in formulae of paradox that illuminate in poetic flashes the long and much controversial history of Christological dogma:

> Vergine Madre, figlia del tuo figlio,
>   umile e alta più che creatura,
>   termine fisso d'etterno consiglio,
> tu sei' colei che l'umana natura
>   nobilitasti sì che' l tuo fattore
>   non disdegnò di farsi sua fattura.
> Nel ventre tuo si raccese l'amore
>   per lo cui caldo ne l'etterna pace
> così è germinato questo fiore.
>   (*Par.* XXXIII, 1-9)

Next, it is Mary the womanly intercessor who is praised as "so great and of such worth that if anyone wanting grace does not run to thee, his is a longing that wants to fly without wings." And then, at last, comes the particularized prayer on Dante's behalf, calling upon Mary to scatter every cloud of Dante's mortality with her own prayers so that he may experience the ultimate happiness for which our souls are made and yet not suffer destruction of his human sensibilities and affections.

Mary's eyes, beloved and venerated by God, make the final vision possible. At the beginning of Paradiso, Dante — we need to recall — had warned those who were following him in "piccioletta barca" through the Inferno and Purgatorio to turn back for safety, for he was about to set course on waters that poetic art had never before crossed ("l'acqua ch'io prendo già mai non si corse." [*Par.* II, 7]). Theologians and philosophers who have hungrily strained their necks to feed on the bread of angels might safely follow, provided they kept to his furrow, close behind, before the divided waters rushed back to fill it. Is the result of Dante's daringly new artistic voyage[26] to be some vaguely suggestive, orientalized symbolic representation of God's overhanging heavens? Not in the least; for Dante has perfected himself, with Virgil, in the highest skills of pagan classical art and has tapped its highest sources of imagination:

> Minerva spira, e conducemi Appollo,
>   e nove Muse mi dimostran l'Orse.
>   (*Par.* II, 8-9)

The skills of Homeric and Virgilian art can raise an inspired Christian poet very high but not, Dante assures us, high enough. He prays to Mary full of grace for what more he needs to complete his "poema sacro/al qual ha posto mano e cielo e terra" (*Par.* XXV, 1-2). With that deceptively simple phrase, Dante sums up his daring *ars poetica*, fully conscious of his success in giving masterful expression to art on the verge of transcending itself.

In Hegelian terms, Dante's *Commedia* is the perfection of romantic art as distinguished from symbolic and classical art, the characteristic principles of which it includes in a higher synthesis. The three kinds of art are most meaningfully distinguished according to the diverse possible relations that may obtain between artistic intuition and expression, content and form. Classical art, with its perfect adequacy of content and form, holds the middle place. But art can do more as well as less than what the classical perfectionists attempted. In Hegel's concise formulation: "Symbolic art *seeks* that perfect unity of inner meaning and external shape which classical art *finds* in the presentation of substantial individuality to sensuous contemplation, and which romantic art *transcends* in its superior spirituality." (Knox, p. 302) Clarifying his aesthetic use of the term *transcends*, he adds with precision: "Romantic art is the self-transcendence of art but within its own sphere and in the form of art itself." (Knox, p. 80)

Dante, we may say in conclusion, is the first poet of the West (and in some respects perhaps also the last) to recognize the absolute limits of art, right up to the highest source of inspiration, which through Mary's intercession, takes him into the blinding light of divine love, where being, beauty, truth, and goodness transcend themselves together. In the *Commedia*, he indeed managed (as he proposed at the beginning of the Paradiso) to run art's entire course. And we may best sum up the point of our discussion by noting that for Hegel's definition of the distinctive character of romantic-Christian aesthetic consciousness not less than for Dante's consummate realization of that consciousness in a work of art, a high appreciation of the powers of Marian inspiration (if not quite a cult of Mary *Theotókos*) was indispensable.

NOTES

1. Daisy Fornacca Kouzel, "The Hegelian Influence in the Literary Criticism of Francesco De Sanctis," *Review of National Literatures*, I, 2 (Fall 1970), 214-231. See also: Daisy Fornacca, *Hegel, hegeliani, e la letteratura italiana: variazioni su temi di Hegel* (Firenze: Società Editrice Universitaria, 1952).

2. G.W.F. Hegel, *Aesthetics: Lectures on Fine Art*, trans. T.M. Knox (2 vols. Oxford: The Clarendon Press, 1975). (All references to this translation will hereafter be given in the text.) For earlier translations, see *The Philosophy of Fine Art*, F.P.B. Osmaston (4

vols. London: G. Bell and Sons, 1920) and *The Introduction to Hegel's Philosophy of Fine Art,* Bernard Bosanquet (London, K. Paul, Trench, Trübner, 1903).

3. Bosanquet, *A History of Aesthetic* (London, Allen and Unwin, 1892 [1966]), p. 167.

4. *Ibid.,* p. 168.

5. *Ibid.,* pp. 169-170.

6. *Dante Alighieri Epistolae,* ed. and trans. By Paget Toynbee (Oxford: The Clarendon Press, 1920), p. 202.

7. See Olof Lagercrantz, *From Hell to Paradise: Dante and His Comedy,* trans. Alan Blair (New York, Washington Square Press, 1966), pp. 86ff.

8. Here and throughout I cite the critical edition of Giorgio Petrocchi, *La Commedia second l'antica vulgata* (4 vol. Milano, Mondatori, 1966-67). Unless otherwise indicated, where I offer translations from Dante, they are my own, incorporating, of course, phrases that many of the major translators have long since wisely adopted from one another as unavoidably appropriate.

9. Milano: Casale Monferrato, 1960.

10. See Knox, pp. 69-90, 517-552, and *passim* (especially index entries under *Dante, Mary, romantic art*).

11. Author's adaptation. For the German text, see George Wilhelm Friedrich Hegel, *Aesthetik,* nach der zweiten Ausgabe Heinrich Gustav Hothos (1842) redigiert . . .von Friedrich Bassange (2 vols.; Berlin and Weimar: Aufbau-Verlag, 1965), Vol. I, p. 422. See also: Knox, pp. 437-438. Both author's adaptations and the Knox translation are based on the Bassenge edition of the Hothos text.

12. Bosanquet, trans., *Introduction,* p. 184. Cf. *Hegel on Tragedy,* ed. Anne and Henry Paolucci (New York, Doubleday & Sons, 1972; Harper and Row, 1975), pp. xix-xxiv. New edition, (Griffon House Publications (Smyrna Delaware and New York, 2001).

13. Adolf von Harnack, *History of Dogma,* trans, Neil Buchanan (7 vols., New York: Russell and Russell, 1958), Vol. IV, p. 321. (See Vol. IV, pp. 317-330.)

14. Adapted. Cf. Bassenge, pp. 514-515; Knox, p. 535.

15. Slightly adapted. Cf. Bassenge, p. 522; Knox, pp. 542-543.

16. Slightly adapted. Cf. Bassenge, Vol II, 200, 201; Knox, pp.

824-825.

17. Slightly adapted. Cf. Bassenge, Vol. II, 462-463; Knox, pp. 1103-1104.

18. Henry Adams, *Mont Saint Michel and Chartres* (New York, New American Library, 1961), p. 245.

19. *Ibid.*, pp. 245-246.

20. *Ibid.*, pp. 249-250.

21. For a full discussion of Hegel's dematerialization of the arts — as it applies to the Purgatorio — see Anne Paolucci, "Dante's Tribute to the Fine Arts in the *Purgatorio*," *Italica*, XLII, 1: Special Number, "A Homage to Dante" (1965), 42-60. A later version of this article, under the title "Art and Nature in Dante's *Purgatorio*" is included in *Hegelian Literary Perspectives* (Griffon House Publications, Smyrna, Delaware and New York, 2002), pp. 350=365.

22. Adams, p. 245.

23. T.S. Eliot, "What Dante Means to Me," in *To Criticize the Critic* (New York, Farrar, Straus and Giroux, 1965), p. 129.

24. *Ibid,*, p. 132.

25. See: Dino Bigongiari, *Essays on Dante and Medieval Culture* (Firenze: L.S. Olschki, 1964), esp. "Preface" by Henry Paolucci, pp. 5-15; also *New York Times*, Sept, 8, 1965. A new edition of the book was published by Griffon House Press in 2002. A section of Professor Bigongiari's lectures on Dante, "The Political Ideas of St. Augustine" appears in Henry Paolucci's *The Political Writings of St. Augustine* (Chicago. Henry Regnery Co., 1962), pp. 343=358. The full text of Professor Bigongiari's lectures on Dante, edited by Anne and Henry Paolucci, has been published by Griffon House Publications in two separate vbolumes: *Backgrounds of the Divine Comedy* (2005) and *Readings in the Divine Comedy* (2006).

26. For an interpretation of Dante's "altro viaggio," in its moral or tropological significance, that parallels the argument here touched on, see Anne Paolucci, "Exile Among the Exiles: Dante's Party of One," first published in *Mosaic*, VIII, 3 (Spring 1975), 117-123 and included in this volume.

THE STRIDENT VOICES OF HELL

First published as the Introductory essay to Dante's Gallery of Rogues, *containing color prints of 34 paintings of the* Inferno *by Vincenzo R. Latella (Griffon House Publications, Smyrna (Delaware), New York, 2001).*

> "lasciate ogni speranza voi ch'entrate."
> *INFERNO.* III, 9

> "The undiscovered country from whose
> bourn no traveler returns . . . ."
> *HAMLET.* III, 1, 79-80

> "I reached the portal common spirits fear,
> And read the words above it, dark and clear,
> 'Leave hope behind, all ye who enter **here**'."
> James Thomson,
> *THE CITY OF DREADFUL NIGHT*

1. TELLING THE STORY

The well-known mystery writer and enthusiastic critic-translator of *The Divine Comedy*, Dorothy L. Sayers, calls Dante's poem "a story of adventure."[1] It has, she keeps reminding us, all the elements we associate with good narrative: "structure, speed, particularity, style," and "a universe of breathing characters."[2] And, fueling the narrative, a great poetic imagination as well.

Dante had learned a great deal about telling a story from his master, Virgil, and from others like Ovid and Statius; he knew the Vulgate "inside out"; and he had most certainly profited from his close and appreciative reading of the romance writers of the northern tradition.

All this, Sayers tells us, contributed to making Dante "a miraculous story-teller."[3]

He seems fully aware that in telling a story he — the sophisticated poet of the *Vita Nuova* and *Convivio*, of courtly love — has humbled himself, catering to a more general audience. In fact, he had already decided to write his great poem in Italian, the "vulgar" tongue, rather than in Latin — something unheard of at the time for a poem or any work dealing with high philosophy, religion, morality, metaphysics.

Why indeed did a poet so superbly trained, with

67

such experience and skill in such a variety of poetic forms, fully aware that serious works were still written in Latin, that the ""vulgar" was used only for the more common exchanges and for simple love lyrics — why did he deliberately choose to write the *Commedia* in Italian? No answer can satisfy completely, except his own, and that one is not altogether clear. We know he had carefully studied the sixteen major tongues of Italy, examining each in detail, aiming to find the best qualities of each so that they might be combined into one tongue that could perhaps serve the entire peninsula (*De Vulgari Eloquentia*). Whatever his theory, he tested it in the *Commedia*. There the Italian language was shaped and molded to fit the poet's needs. In Dante's hands, it responded with unexpected fluidity, power, and grace. It proved it could indeed tackle that astonishing mix of history, philosophy, politics, preaching, satire, romance, autobiography, and adventure — and in a manner that suggests that the language had been used that way for decades. Actually, Dante was the first to do so.

His "colossal humility" as a story-teller is offset by a "colossal self-confidence"[4] in his overall abilities as a poet. He does not hesitate to admit his own greatness and vote himself into the eternal hall of fame. But then, anything less would have been less than true.

"The structure of the thing is in every way astonishing,"[5] Sayers writes; "the sheer pace is in fact, extraordinary."[6] Although he never forgets that other magic element, which places him apart from so many other excellent story-tellers, Dante "does not assume his singing robes; he merely assumes that he has them on . . . . The poem does not start off like an epic, but with the disarming simplicity of a ballad or a romance or a fairy-tale."[7] This is a significant observation and we will have occasion to see just how extraordinary that beginning is.

2. THE THREE CANTICLES

Dante tells us that his epic poem is a "comedy." He wasn't suggesting the poem was funny, although there is humor in it; what he meant was that the work has a "fortunate" outcome, it ends well. Later commentators added the word "divine," no doubt to express their appreciation of the poem's beauty, but also, perhaps, as a reminder of the journey's goal: salvation. Dante himself refers to the work as "poema sacro" by the time he reaches Paradiso.

The journey described is in three parts. The multifaceted display of the self-serving will is the subject matter of the Inferno. In this first canticle, Dante reviews the ways in which human beings destroy their God-given faculties by indulging their appetites and perverting their judgment. The sinners in Hell have put themselves first in all things. They are forever shut out from the light and love of God. Their vision has not altered, their passions have not diminished. If anything, they are even more assertive, more demanding in their willfulness. At the same time, they see clearly the full implications of their actions, the completed deed, as it were.

The second part of the journey, Purgatorio, is about self-effacement and rehabilitation. In it we witness the purification of the will, which has come to recognize the error of its ways and its innate love for the Good. Purgatorio prepares the soul for the return to God. Here the penitents are not the assertive personalities of Hell; they are unobtrusive participants in a therapeutic program meant to refine their sensibilities and hone their talents. For Purgatorio is a great hymn to the fine arts, peopled with musicians, poets, artists, as they express the beauty and goodness of God. Dante seduces us with the best in art, then moves beyond art to reconstituted nature, nature restored to its pristine beauty at the very top of Purgatorio. All that, he reminds us, will disappear on the day of judgment, when Purgatorio and everything in it, all the arts and the new Eden, will be absorbed into Paradiso.

In the final cantos of Purgatorio, the reconstituted will, purified through a new Baptism, Confession, and Absolution; strengthened by the allegorical pageant depicting the history of Christianity and Holy Church, from the beginning right up to Dante's time; having witnessed the destructive confrontation between universal Church and universal Empire, is now prepared to enter the mysteries of Paradiso.

This third canticle educates us emotionally and in every other way for the sight of the Holy Trinity and God. But Dante warns us more than once that our spiritual eyes must be made strong to withstand the vision of the Godhead. To make his point, he introduces us along the way to the saints, theologians, and martyrs, whose manifest love for God shines in and through them. Not surprisingly, the Paradiso is also a refresher course in theology, dogma, and the mysteries of Faith, even *explication de texte*, as in the beautiful rendering of the "Hail Mary" by St. Bernard. Mary, in fact, is the final intermediary between Dante and the vision of the triune God. Beatrice has slipped away, leaving Dante in St. Bernard's care. It is he, the devoted advocate of Mary, who intercedes for Dante now.

Paradiso is an ever-more challenging theological and spiritual illumination. There is no vestige here of worldly beauty, history, art, or reconstituted nature. Everything has been transformed. Dante alerts us to the difficulty of describing this phase of the journey by using a wealth of similes and other images that suggest what is in final analysis an experience beyond the senses, beyond the grasp of our merely human faculties.

3. THE POLITICAL THESIS

One large reason for the astounding response Dante continues to elicit through the centuries, from the time of Boccaccio (the first to take on the poem in a series of lectures in Florence), down to our own day, is that the struggle Dante described continues in one form or another, its power undiminished. His message about social chaos and personal damnation, and the connection between the two, carries down to our own age.

Dante wrote his epic poem during his political exile, which began in 1302 and lasted until his death in Ravenna in 1321. He was driven from Florence by petty power-politics. Accused of barratry, he refused to pay the fine imposed on him, knowing himself to be innocent of the charge, and chose not to recognize the ruling of the Court. His refusal to submit to the sentence and to recognize the duly constituted authority that had passed judgment on him, forced his peers to sentence him to permanent exile with the threat of death should he ever set foot in his native city again.

Against Dante's own personal political difficulties is the large power struggle which is the burden of the poem: the destructive confrontation between the supporters of imperial rule and those of the Pope, a struggle which fuels Dante's treatise, *De Monarchia (On World Government)*, and which we hear about in a variety of poetic refrains throughout the *Commedia.*

For Dante, the need for separate and distinct temporal and spiritual leadership in the world is essential and basic. The *Commedia* is built on this assumption. It weaves its way in and out of the poem in recurring motifs. The matter is barely touched on in the opening canto, but Dante's encounters with Farinata, Ugolino and others in Inferno and elsewhere are variations of that theme, creating a cumulative and powerful effect. At the very center of the earth, where Satan has been thrust from the heavens, the theme reaches one of its most memorable expressions.

But perhaps the most direct account of the political question is in Canto XVI of Purgatorio. The passage should be noted here, not only as an excellent illustration of Dante's command of the architectural structure he has devised, the topography which enables him to minimize moral explanations, but also as the brief but unforgettable genesis of the political ills of the world, seen in historical and philosophical perspective. Here the wrathful are being punished; but, as usual, Dante soon draws our attention elsewhere. The first thing we discover is that we have reached the precise midpoint of the poem, the fiftieth of 100 cantos. What this tells us is that the passage in question is centrally located and therefore of central importance. (Once we understand how Dante works these techniques, we begin to look for more and we are rarely disappointed.)

In this instance, Virgil has asked Dante to inquire if they are indeed going in the right direction (unlike similar encounters in Inferno, no one here will try to mislead them). Dante accordingly addresses one of the penitents. The man who responds tells him, in four tight lines, that his name is Marc, that he is from Lombardy, where he followed virtue and goodness, that he made every effort to uphold those values that everyone is now bent on destroying, and, yes, they're on the right track.

But Marc's mention of virtue and values has made Dante forget his usual modesty, and he blurts out another question that is bothering him: "Tell me, why has the world lost those values you and others hold dear?" Tell me, so I can report back to the others left behind, because some people insist the cause of evil and disorder is to be found in the influence of the stars, others that it's here among us, our doing. Marc sighs, but answers. And that answer has become one of the high points of the poem, for in addition to anticipating the lovely description of the guileless Wordsworthian soul seeking its Maker from the moment of its birth, in addition to a magnificent poetic account of the Platonic ladder of love, it also gives us an unforgettable political thesis on the need to separate temporal and spiritual authority if mankind is to find its way back to God. It is an important moral and political landmark of the *Commedia* but also one of the most beautiful poetic passages ever written.

Marc Lombard first answers Dante's question about free will. Even to ask the question shows how blind men have become, he tells Dante bluntly. Down there you all think that things happen of necessity. If that were the case, you would have no choices, there would be no reason to rejoice in the good and avoid evil. At first, it's hard, he says; but you have in you the power to seek freedom and better things:

> . . . the world is blind;
> and you must come from there.
> You, the living, trace all causes

to the stars, as though they draw
things after them by necessity.
If this were so, free will would be destroyed in you
and there would be no just reason for rejoicing
in goodness and grieving over evil.
The stars first spur you into action —
I don't say all action, but even if I did,
you have a light that shows you good from bad,
and free will, which if it stands firm
through the first battles with the stars,
will win out in the end, if nourished properly.
Free will leads to a greater force a better nature
and creates in you the mind over which
the stars have no control.
Therefore, if the world has gone astray,
the cause is in yourselves, in you the question lies,
as I will now truthfully reveal to you.[8]

(. . . [l]o mondo è cieco, e tu vien ben da lui.
Voi che vivete ogni cagion recate
    per suso al cielo, pur come se tutto
    movesse seco di necessitate.
Se così fosse, in voi fora distrutto
    libero arbitrio, e non fora giustizia,
    per ben letizia, e per male aver lutto.
Lo ciel i vostri movimenti inizia, —
    non dico tutti, ma posto ch' i 'l dica,
    lume v' è dato a bene e a malizia,
e libero voler, che, se fatica
    ne le prime battaglie col ciel dura,
    poi vince tutto, se ben si notrica.
A maggior forza e a miglior natura
    liberi soggiacete, e quella cria
    la mente in voi, che 'l ciel non ha in sua cura.
Però, se 'l mondo presente disvia,
    In voi è la cagione, in voi si cheggia
    Ed io te ne sarò or vera spia.)[9]

Having assured Dante that our free will, not the stars or
the influences of nature, is the final arbiter in all choices,
Marc Lombard gives this beautiful account of the newly-
created soul seeking the things that give it joy, in its
unconscious and natural effort to return to the source of
its happiness:

From his hand, who delights in her
even before she comes into being,
the simple new-born soul, like a little maid

plays, weeping and laughing, knowing
nothing except that, moved by her happy maker,
she willingly returns to that which gives her joy.
First she finds pleasure in a tiny good;
misled, she rushes after it,
unless held back or someone
turn her from that love.

(Esce di mano a lui che la vagheggia
   prima che sia — a guisa di fanciulla
   che piangendo e ridendo pargoleggia —
l'anima semplicetta, che sa nulla,
   salvo che, mossa da lieto fattore,
   volentier torna a ciò che la trastulla.
Di picciol bene in pria sente sapore;
   quivi s'inganna, e dietro ad esso corre,
   se guida o fren non torce suo amore.)

To guide the innocent, naive soul in its first automatic
response toward the things that give it joy, some measure
of control must be applied. At this point Marc Lombard
introduces the major theme:

Therefore laws had to be found to act as brakes,
a king had to be found who could discern at least
the towers of the true city.
We have the laws, but who enforces them?
No one; for the shepherd who leads the way
can meditate but lacks the cloven hoof.[10]
And those who follow, seeing their leader
reach for those goods they themselves desire,
settle for them and ask for nothing more.
You can well see that evil leadership
is the cause of the world's ills
not nature corrupted in you.
Rome, that made the good world,
once had two suns, lighting one and another road,
that of the world and that of God.
One has put out the other;
and the sword is joined with the crozier;
together they can only do damage
because thus joined one does not fear the other.
If you don't believe me, think of an ear of corn,
how every fruit is known by its seed.

(Onde convenne legge per fren porre;
   convenne rege aver, che discernesse
   de la vera città almen la torre.
Le leggi son, ma chi pon mano ad esse?

Nullo; però che 'l pastor che precede
rugumar può, ma non ha l' ungie fesse.
Per che la gente, che sua guida vede
   pur a quel ben ferire ond' ella è ghiotta,
   di quel si pasce, e più oltre non chiede.
Ben puoi veder che la mala condotta
   è la cagion che 'l mondo ha fatto reo,
   e non natura che 'n voi sia corrotta.
Soleva Roma, che 'l buon mondo feo,
   due soli aver, che 'l una e l' altra strada
   facean veder, e del mondo e di Deo.
L' un l' altro ha spento, ed è giunta la spada
   col pastorale; e l' un con l' altro insieme
   per viva forza mal convien che vada,
Però che giunti, l 'un l' altro non teme.
   Se non mi credi, pon mente alla spiga,
   ch' ogn' erba si conosce per lo seme.)

There's more before the canto comes to an end,
but these passages should suffice. Dante makes very clear
that the world has gone astray because the papal crozier
and the imperial sword have come together, thereby
destroying the delicate balance of the two sources of
power, temporal and spiritual, without which man
cannot hope to find salvation.

This will be the major theme of the Inferno and
the burden of the entire poem. Three centuries later, in a
similar situation, another Florentine, Niccolo Machiavelli, will take on many of the same arguments to
produced a powerful practical manifesto on *realpolitik*:
The Prince.

IV. THE REALM OF SATAN
General Comments

Inferno is the most dramatic and richest
reflection of this political, social, and religious chaos. It is
also the place where the most assertive political voices
are heard justifying their partisan attitudes. The sinners
have lost their moral bearings because of their self-
indulgence; and they are held responsible for their
conduct, because free will, God's great gift to mankind,
has been turned toward self-gratification. But Dante
never lets us forget that the Pope and the Emperor are

also responsible for having betrayed their trust, their great office as leaders. They have failed in their given task to protect and guide mankind, each in his own way, according to God's grand design.

This and other themes are set within an architectural and topographical design that is itself a poetic statement. It also allows Dante tremendous economy with words, since the structure is itself a moral and spiritual statement.

In Paradiso, Dante sets his meetings and interviews against the familiar astronomical heavens, in order to dismiss in an impressive way the notion that the will is in any important way subject to the influence of the stars and planets. In Purgatorio, the ledges on the mountain represent the traditional sins and provide us with artistic exemplars to soothe and encourage the soul in its journey of expiation. But in Inferno, where there is neither light nor stars nor recognizable landmarks to go by, the very structure must guide us. Dante must create an environment that needs no large explanation, that speaks for itself as we move further and deeper into it. The result is an extraordinary roadmap.

The Circles of Hell

Inferno is a huge cavity shaped like an inverted truncated cone, widest at the top, narrowing to almost a point at the center of the earth, where Dante and Virgil will slowly move, to emerge into the open again, finally, to see the stars and work their way to the mountain of Purgatorio.

The entire cavernous area of Inferno is divided into nine circles or ledges of different widths and characteristics, where sinners are relegated for all eternity with ingenious punishments created by Dante the poet to fit the sin both morally and poetically. The circles or ledges are separated from one another by cliffs of varying steepness and height. Two enormous precipices divide it roughly into three horizontal sections. A huge wall circling one of the terraces cuts the outermost section from the other two, creating an Upper and Lower Hell — the latter also known as The City of Dis.

In the upper part of Hell are those who sinned against nature. The sins of excesses are familiar and appear again and again in traditional literature and in church manuals: lust, gluttony, avarice and prodigality, anger, and (perhaps to mark the transition into the lower regions) the sin of heresy. At this point, the walls of Dis rise up to separate this first large area from the second narrower one, where the violent are punished. The descent into the area of the fraudulent is steep and difficult, every step a real danger and threat. Beyond this narrow area, or rather at the very center of it, stuck there, filling up what remains of the opening, is the beastly figure of Satan himself.

The Topography or Moral Geography of Hell

By setting up his place for the damned within an inverted truncated cone set in the middle of the earth, Dante is already speaking allegorically and morally. Utter darkness tells us, without need for explanations, that this is a place where we can easily lose ourselves, since there are no familiar guidelines or landmarks to follow. Darkness also denotes the absence of light; and in Dante's moral universe (as in that of Aeschylus, Milton, and so many others), light is synonymous with knowledge, illumination, insight. All these are missing where there is darkness. The very geography of the place tells us quickly that we are growing more and more restricted in our movements, in our ability to step from moment to moment, from ledge to ledge, without error, without danger. Finally, marking the dead-end or *cul-de-sac,* which is the very bottom of the pit, Lucifer corks up the opening, all that remains of Hell. Dante has created an ingenious architectural structure that speaks for itself.

The effect of the closing in of the walls as we move down into the darkness of Hell, intensified by the increasing cold, the sounds and smells that assail us, the anger rage and frustration of the inhabitants of the place, the visual images drained of all humanity, tell us in unambiguous language that Hell is the place where freedom and love have forever been lost and those who inhabit it have been made painfully aware of that loss.

Satan

"I did not die, I did not remain alive," Dante tells us[11] at the sight of Satan. He insists on telling us how difficult it is to approximate that terrible sight, to find the proper words to describe it, but of course, in so doing he is giving us both the measure of the difficulty and the extent of his success. He succeeds primarily by using familiar symbolic allusions to highlight Satan's condition and that of the traitors who will be joined to him for all eternity. Dante's imagery at this point in the poem reinforces the notion of bestiality, or more properly, of a new sub-human species created by the fall from grace. Satan is described in language that brings to mind the ugliest features of animals. He has three heads: the one in front is red; the one on the right is a yellowish white; the left one is black. Directly below these, two huge bat-like winds move slowly, creating the cold wind and ice of Cocytus.

In his powerfully evocative clusters of images Dante quickly is able to impress upon us that Satan is a fallen super-being who, in his betrayal of God, was transformed into a sub-human being, something quite new and awful, one of a kind. He is not a mere animal, for animals are created by God to serve a good purpose. Neither is he simply *in*human, for he was never human to begin with. Everything about him is unnatural, repulsive, disgusting, ugly, perverted. His outward appearance is nothing we can relate to; it is an invention of Dante's. But we have no doubt as to what this caricature or monster represents. His frustrated tears, dripping from three pairs of eyes over three chins, coming together with gore and bloody foam drooling from each of three mouths, where he chomps at the sinners trapped in them, his clawing, which strips the skin off their backs again and again, his relentless biting, crushing their bodies between his teeth, torturing them in whatever way possible and within his power, is the only way Satan is able to give vent to his unrelieved frustration, his mighty rage. He is in himself the embodiment of the impotence represented by Hell.

The Arch-Traitors: Brutus, Cassius, and Judas

All around that small opening, embedded in what appear to be sheets of glass, are the worst of all sinners, those who have betrayed their lords and masters, who have destroyed the most intimate trust between human beings. They are visible through the transparent surface of ice like bits of straw, in all kinds of positions, some standing, some back to back, head to head, some bent, completely covered by the ice.

But it is the three sinners in Satan's grasp that draw Dante's special attention. Dante the Poet has put them there, and for a good reason; Dante the Narrator has to discover them there and make them part of the story he is telling. And by this time, we can recognize without too much explanation both the terrible betrayal they have committed and the large consequences of that betrayal.

Hanging from the black muzzle, Virgil explains, is Brutus; hanging from the yellowish mouth is Cassius. The one in the middle mouth, whose head is hidden inside the moving red jaws and whose legs are dangling below, is Judas Iscariot. No great surprise, once we grasp that, for Dante, Brutus and Cassius are not the heroic defenders of the Roman Republic but the arch-traitors who killed Julius Caesar and tried to prevent the launching of the Roman Empire. That Empire came finally into being; and under the great Augustus Caesar, Virgil himself was born. As for Judas Iscariot, the betrayer of Christ and the Universal Church, Virgil does nothing more than identify him. No further explanations are necessary. The rest of the traitors in that hell-hole are shown forever embedded in the cold and dark transparency of ice, like insects trapped under a laminated surface. It is the ultimate humiliation, the most painful *reductio* of the human soul to agonizing awareness of its eternal fate.

This entire last scene of Inferno is full of sounds and smells and sights that defy description. Neither Virgil nor Dante say much as they struggle to climb out of the pit of Hell. They must find their way along the ribs of Satan's bat-like wings, holding on for dear life. All kinds of dangers lurk around them and every step threatens to plummet them back into the dark pit. The moral and spiritual implications of this moment are clear enough but cannot be minimized. If Dante survives, it is only because, on another level of being, his future has been assured.

The Augustinian View

Coming for the first time to Dante's bestial Satan from the eloquent "Byronic hero" of Milton's *Paradise Lost*, T. S. Eliot was honest enough to note that many English readers might take away from the last Canto of Inferno "the impression of a Devil suffering like the human damned souls" an impression that makes us keenly aware of the contrast between the two representations and forces upon us the conclusion that "the *kind* of suffering experienced by the Spirit of Evil," as described by Dante, "should be represented as utterly different."[12]

Eliot, as one might expect, eventually comes around to correct this initial impression. For it is certainly not the impression Dante wishes to leave with us; or rather, it *is* an impression he wishes to produce — but properly understood. What he describes is the draining of all goodness and light and love.

In this dark hole, in the very center of the earth, there is barely a vestige of God left. There is nothing heroic about Dante's Satan, nothing even remotely glamorous about his indomitable will. He can't even get a simple word out, let alone indulge in the kind of lofty diatribes Milton's Satan is allowed. The noise of his gnawing on bone and gristle, the movement of his huge bat-like wings, which produce the icy winds that freeze Cocytus, are far removed from any vestige of Lucifer's former grandeur.

Still, Eliot is right in registering disappointment at first. All of us conditioned by Milton's Satan have to readjust our sights when we come to Dante. In the topography of Hell it is not difficult to do so. We are in No Man's Land, in a rocky cavern situated in the bowels of the earth; nothing compares to this place. And once our eyes have adjusted, we realize that the punishment of

Satan is indeed *qualitatively* different. The full horror bears down on us as we take in the sub-human transformation he has suffered. No other sinner has been subjected to anything like it. The constricting claustrophobic space; the nature of the beast — a one-of-a-kind monster — his awful aspect, the travesty of the divine trinity in the three horrible heads resting on one pair of shoulders, are all part of an ingenious unique description. To further understand the moral implications of all this, we should remember that in Canto XI of Inferno Dante reviews his outline, scraps his early design based on familiar transgressions, and announces an Augustinian buttressing for the rest of the Inferno.

The large upper circles of the incontinent, those who allowed the natural appetites to rule them, giving in to excesses, are followed by the circles of the violent and those of the fraudulent. Not only does this give Dante a chance to express more vividly his views on political matters, personal and public fraud and the like; it also dramatizes a much more profound theory, namely, that sin is not something substantive in itself but the emptiness, the squalor if you like, that comes with the absence of God's goodness and love. As we approach the very bottom of the pit, space grows more and more constricted, human attributes are more and more reduced to bestial sounds, normal exchanges become curses and invectives. We see nature undergoing a terrible transformation, both in the beings stuck in these places and in the barren rocky places themselves. Dante is draining the earth of everything good in it. This is surely symbolic but also real. The place reeks, the sounds are moans and curses, the sky is invisible and will continue to be hidden until the difficult journey into the bowels of the earth is over.

Still, even a vestige of life, no matter how misdirected, contains a measure of the divine by the sheer fact of its existence. And, Satan himself, so long as he can move his bat-like wings, shed his tears of frustration, so long as he 'metes out punishment on the arch-traitors, gnawing their bodies, is asserting the power and glory of

God. In his own way and under the circumstances described, Satan in fact rules as king. For Dante never lets us forget that the City of Dis belongs to Satan as the other City belongs to God.

One other technique needs to be mentioned. Dante highlights special moments in decidedly unusual ways. In this case, he does what he will do again at the top of Purgatorio and Paradiso, both critical moments like this one. He describes through a rich collection of similes his inability to tell us accurately what he saw and felt: he describes his confusion, his disorientation, the darkness and heavy fog, which reduce visibility almost to zero, the sense of imminent danger. He stumbles and stutters in trying to make sense of all this; and we are alerted by his insistence on this difficulty to the double transcendence he is in fact illustrating: his admission that both words and memory fail him at this point, that we are witnessing an *ecstatic* experience.

All this is part of a subtle and masterful technique, of course. Its effect is cumulative, enriched by the juxtaposition of opposites, clusters or families of images that together produce a vivid and unforgettable impression. All this against the Augustinian backdrop of God's presence in all things, even in the most despicable of sinners.

Seen as the dark antithesis of the light and love of God, Dante's Satan cannot fail to produce an impression at least as forceful as that produced by the "Byronic hero" of Milton's epic poem. The poetic language of the last canto of Inferno is no less dramatic than the language of *Paradise Lost*. Dante, with the sensitive touch of a true poet, recalls the main theme in a powerful minor key, using discordant notes and jarring sounds, silences even, to suggest the full exhaustion of the lyrical melody. For it is in the fullness of the poem seen and heard in all its architectural diversity, its echoing naves and its musical choirs, that every part is enriched.

The Inferno is the destructiveness of self-love, the negation of *caritas*, and Dante's Satan is the extreme expression of that self-love, asserting itself against God, cut off forever from happiness, love, and freedom. Dante depicts the fallen angel's loss of freedom as a genial allegorical transparency of constricted space. The huge monster is forever stuck in the hole he has created, barely able to move. In spite of title as "lo imperador del doloroso regno,"[13] he is truly prisoner in his own realm.

Eliot finally came to understand and appreciate this Satan as an integral and organic part of Dante's vision, drawn with the same memorable strokes which make the last canto of Paradiso, where the scattered pages of the universe are bound in one volume — in Eliot's words — "the highest point that poetry has ever reached or ever can reach."[14]

Unanswered Questions

The number three and multiples of three serve in important ways in the *Commedia*. There are nine circles in Inferno, nine heavens in Paradiso. There are three canticles each containing thirty-three cantos, with the exception of Inferno, which has an extra "introductory" canto, bringing the total number of cantos in the poem to a magic 100. We saw how the number three evokes more than once the Holy Trinity, even in the pit of hell; and without going into a long discourse on numerology and what Dante and his contemporaries believed with respect to the special meaning of numbers, we can safely say that he was well versed in the subject and made good use of it in his poem. In the opening canto of Inferno, we are immediately faced with a threesome, symbolic beasts that represent the sins of mankind.

This first canto and the one that follows not only provide the blueprint for what is to come, they also introduce us to the narrator, Dante the Florentine, Dante the man, who has just experienced a terrible ordeal and can hardly begin to speak about it.

Dante, the extraordinary story-teller, begins by recalling his breathless escape from a dark wood. He is full of fear, his heart pounding at the mere thought of what he had endured there. He doesn't go into details.

He doesn't have to. He is telling his listeners to fill in whatever it is that they've experienced in that way, whatever terrors have plagued them. We are already in a scenario in which Dante is also Everyman.

He tells us all this happened in the middle of his life, which means he was thirty-five at the time, half the biblical seventy considered then, as now, the natural span of life. We learn soon enough that it is Good Friday of the year 1300 (the entire journey covers that one weekend). The opening lines set the fast pace and the horror and mystery which characterize the Inferno.

> In the middle of life's journey,
> I found myself in a dark wood,
> the right path completely lost.
> Ah, to tell about that savage, harsh, thick wood
> is a hard task, the very thought renews my fear!
> So bitter, death is hardly more;
> But to deal with the good I found in there,
> I must relate the other things I saw.

> (Nel mezzo del cammin di nostra vita
>   mi ritrovai per una selva oscura,
>   chè la dirritta via era smarrita.
> Ah quanto a dir qual era è cosa dura
>   esta selva selvaggia e aspra e forte,
>   che nel pensier rinnova la paura!
> Tant' è amara che poco è più morte;
>   ma per trattar del ben ch' io vi trovai,
>   dirò de l' altre cose ch' io v' ho scorte.)

Having established the mood, having introduced the mystery, he rushes on to bring us into the present while still lingering on the nightmare experience he has referred to. In these lines, Dante is speaking clearly as the protagonist rather than the narrator. He is telling us how he personally went astray. The words he uses are transparent and direct; we can easily grasp the implications and connotations of *dark, thick wood* or *forest, sleep, the right path*, and so on. Without for a moment breaking through the delicate poetic fabric, he describes in the simplest language an experience that is anything but simple.

> I can't really tell how I got there,
> I was so full of sleep at that point

where I left the true road.
Then coming to the foot of a hill
where that valley ended that had filled
my heart with fear,
I looked up and saw its shoulders
already draped in the rays of the planet
that everywhere leads men to the right path.
Then the fear that had flooded
my heart all through the night
so piteously spent, subsided somewhat.
And as one who comes from the sea panting
on to the shore, looks back
to stare at the dangerous waters,
so my soul, still running, turned to look
at the place no living soul
had ever left before.

(Io non so ben ridir com' io v' entrai;
      tant' era pieno di sonno a quel punto
      che la verace via abbandonai.
Ma poi ch' i' fui al piè d' un colle giunto,
      là dove terminava quella valle
      che m' avea di paura il cor compunto,
guardai in alto, e vidi le sue spalle
      vestite già de' raggi del pianeta
      che mena dritto altrui per ogni calle.
Allor fu la paura un poco queta
      che nel lago del cor n' era durata
      la notte ch' io passai con tanta pieta.
E come quei che, con lena affannata,
      uscito fuor del pelago a la riva,
      si volge a l' acqua perigliosa e guata,
così l' animo mio, ch' ancor fuggiva,
      si volse a rietro a rimirar lo passo
      che non lasciò già mai persona viva.)

Quickly Dante gets his bearings and starts walking across the deserted area toward the mountain whose top is already bathed in morning light, but suddenly, out of nowhere, three beasts appear in his path. The first is a leopard, the symbol of all human lusts and cravings; the second is a lion, the symbol of pride; the third is a she-wolf, thin with unappeased cravings, and of the three the most relentless in preventing Dante's progress. Whatever hope Dante may have had of finding a new path out of that deserted place after the ordeal of the night and the terrors of the dark wood is shattered by this third beast, who keeps circling around him, forcing him backwards, toward the dark wood. This third beast, most critics agree, represents corrupt political ambitions, the ineffectual leadership that blocks the road to salvation.

> The restless beast brought new terror
> as it approached me, forcing me back
> little by little to where the sun is silent.

> (Tal mi fece la bestia senza pace,
>   che' venendomi incontro, a poco a poco
>   mi ripigneva la dove 'l sol tace.)

"Forcing me back . . . to where the sun is silent." In one small phrase Dante has set the measure of the poetic suggestivity which will be maintained throughout the poem. Where is it that "il sol tace"? The dark wood, of course. The beast is pushing him back into the place from which he has just escaped, the place where there is no sun to speak to him, to tell him what direction to take, where to go. And the sun, of course, is the symbol of God, of knowledge, of illumination; and therefore where the sun is silent there is no possibility of pursuing knowledge or the will of God. The allegorical implications are clear and familiar, but the oxymoron Dante uses, the image of the silent sun, is unexpected and genial.

We never learn exactly how Dante managed to get past the first two beasts — no doubt he is telling us that he was able on his own, with discipline and prayer, to control his appetites and curb his pride — but the third beast is more than he can handle. He needs help. And it is at this moment that Virgil appears. At first Dante doesn't know who it is. All he knows is someone, thank God, is there to help him. He cries out to the stranger. All this in just a few tight lines.

Virgil identifies himself and asks what one might expect him to ask: "Why are you going back there, after all you've been through? Why don't you climb the mountain in front of you?"

The drama that follows is, again, a personal one. Dante, wide-eyed, stunned by the utterly unexpected appearance of the great poet who was his life-long poetic guide and mentor, the poet who shaped his own new style, can only respond with surprise and questions. Only when identities have been established and proper praise bestowed on the great poet of Rome, does Dante refer to the beast still blocking his path. At this point, Virgil quickly moves into the major business at hand, which after all has already been decided elsewhere. He is not there casually. Nor can he urge Dante to climb that sunny mountain directly. Dante is programmed for something else.

He must go another way, on another journey for which he, Virgil, will act as his guide, until someone else will take over. In lines 112-123 he gives a thumbnail sketch of the horrors of Hell they are about to experience vicariously; and he ends by explaining why he can't go further than what has been established, since he is a pagan, relegated to Limbo. Dante, exhilarated and full of new hope and trust, quickly agrees to follow his beloved Virgil.

Not until the second canto does Dante question his having been chosen for this special journey through the afterlife. He must have answers before he can feel confident. And so he asks Virgil: Why me? I'm not Aeneas, who founded Rome; I'm not Paul, who gave the early Church the strength it needed. Those two were shown the realms of the dead for reasons that are pretty obvious. I, Dante, will look foolish, presumptuous even, in taking on such an important undertaking.

And here the poem takes a new turn: Dante now becomes Everyman, as well as the Narrator and the Protagonist of the poem. Because, as Virgil explains, Dante indeed has a divinely ordained mission. Virgil's appearance was not an accident. From the very top of Paradiso, the Blessed Mother herself took the initiative and called upon Lucy — the patron saint of sight, vision, eyes, illumination, enlightenment — to rescue Dante; Lucy, in turn, sought out Beatrice, who actually went down into Limbo, the place where Aeneas resided, and with tears in her eyes, pleaded for his help in saving her faithful lover. The personal journey becomes an epic one.

Perhaps it is the intervention of these three holy women, through Beatrice, that enables Dante to overcome the three beasts. We hear no more about them. Beatrice ends her little speech to Virgil with the first deep chord of what will be one of the major themes of the poem: *Love*.

Love moved me, makes me speak.

(Amor mi mosse, che mi fa parlare.)

Love of God is what moves the stars and the other planets. Love of Goodness is what enables the penitents in Purgatorio to bear their punishment willingly. Misguided love is what brought Paolo and Francesca to their romantic hell.

This is another incredible moment, in which we are lulled, distracted into thinking that everything finally has been straightened out. Not really. Dante, inspired by the fact that Beatrice has taken it upon herself to plead for him with Virgil, glosses over the fact that his big question remains unanswered. True, Beatrice nudged by Lucy, who was called to do what she did by the Virgin Mary, gives Dante the faith he needs to go on. But not until the very top of Purgatorio, when Dante the Protagonist reappears briefly for his new baptism, his spiritual *vita nuova*, his reunion with Beatrice (who has just replaced Virgil), is the extent and importance of his mission finally made clear. He is to observe carefully the historical pageant before him, Beatrice tells him, and to record it faithfully in his memory so that he can report what he has seen and heard back to the world that lives ill. His mission has a purpose that is more than personal salvation.

Dante's initial humility seems to have given way to more than a touch of arrogance. In fact, here and elsewhere, his own standards and preferences seem to be the true measure of things. In his encounter with Beatrice, two-thirds of the way into the poem, it is clear not only that Dante has a great mission ordained by heaven itself, but he personally will be saved (something anathema in Catholic doctrine). He has as the guardian of Purgatorio Cato, a pagan and a suicide. Throughout the ledges of Purgatorio, and elsewhere, he draws examples from pagan as well as Christian sources. The presence of Virgil himself may raise some questions in this context.

Moreover, throughout the Inferno he creates his own ingenious punishments, puts people in places where no one else would have thought they belonged, gives historical basis to events not altogether clear in his own day. In short, he has created places and people that fit nicely into a schemata of his own, especially where political corruption is the subject. We accept all this because it is *consistent*, it is *reasonable*, and, most important, it is *poetically mesmerizing*. Whatever the novelties he introduces, however, Dante never undermines Christian sensibilities.

V. SOME OBSERVATIONS ON DANTE IN AMERICA AND THREE MAJOR BRITISH POETS INFLUENCED BY THE *COMMEDIA*

The list of poets, writers, and scholars who have been drawn to Dante over the centuries is too long to be discussed here (Boccaccio was the first to take on the poem in a series of lectures in Florence); but one must at least mention in this context the tremendous impact Dante had on American literature from the very beginnings of our nation, when a young America was struggling to define its new independent identity.[15] We recall especially that eminent group of Harvard scholars and teachers, at the beginning of the nineteenth century, whose enthusiasm resulted in many excellent translations and valuable scholarly appraisals of Dante's work, as well as later writers, right down to our own time. Even a partial list is impressive: Henry Wadsworth Longfellow, James Russell Lowell, Charles Eliot Norton, Charles H. Grandgent, Allen Tate, Francis Fergusson, Thomas G. Bergin, John Freccero, Charles S. Singleton, Robert Hollander, and perhaps the most eminent of America's Dante scholars and teachers, Dino Bigongiari, who taught at Columbia University for over half a century.

Even more impressive are the innovative readings and interpretations of Dante's lines by other poets. Pre-Raphaelites like William Morris and Dante Gabriel Rossetti were deeply influenced by the idealized figure of Beatrice, who is often the subject of their paintings and verse. Earlier, the greatest of the English Romantic poets, Percy Bysshe Shelley, had come under Dante's spell, giving us, in addition to much else inspired by Dante, a magnificent English translation of one of his favorite passages: the description of the lost paradise, now deserted, and "the solitary lady," the mysterious Matilda, who, at the top of Purgatorio (XXIII, 118-123) comes into view dancing and picking flowers. Her identity in the allegorical structure has never been made clear, but she is recalled by name further on, in Paradiso, XXXIII (118-123). Her appearance in the deserted Garden of Eden is the prelude to the strange pageant that soon comes their way and the appearance of the long-awaited Beatrice, who will replace Virgil as Dante's guide and see her loyal lover safely through the rites of passage that prepare him for the true *vita nuova*.

Shelley's brief excerpt of the Matelda passage is one of the most limpid and beautiful renditions of the Italian text in English.[16] A century later, the Inferno serves as inspiration for James Thomson's *The City of Dreadful Night*, what one critic has called "the most pessimistic poem in English." Thomson actually dedicates his poem to Dante and Leopardi, and opens his *City* with a quotation from the first canto of *Inferno*.

In our own time, it is T. S. Eliot, the American-born British poet, who deserves to be singled out for his life-long appreciation of Dante. In a talk delivered at the Italian Institute in London in 1950, the great poet/critic of our century admitted: "I still, after forty years, regard [Dante's] poetry as the most persistent and deepest influence upon my own verse."[17] This statement, from the author of *The Wasteland*, the most celebrated poem of the twentieth century, confirmed what many critics already had come to realize, that Eliot not only patterned his modern hell after Dante's Inferno, but also used many of Dante's lines and poetic habits in his major poem as well as in other works like "Little Gidding." Eliot's description of the modern world as a Dantesque hell has made the Inferno immediately accessible to readers of our time. *The Wasteland* sums up the existential aftermath of two major wars; it dispels the illusory optimism generated by social reform as the answer to mankind's ills; it strips away false hopes. Like Dante before him, Eliot depicts for us the confusion and despair of a modern secular hell, forcing us, against that bleak reality, to come to terms with our limitations and the world around us.

But Dante says it best, and for all time.

NOTES

1. Dorothy L. Sayers, *Further Papers on Dante* (London, Methuen & Co. Ltd., 1957), p. 10.

2. *Ibid.*, p. 15.

3. *Ibid.*, p. 2.

4. *Ibid.*, p. 7.

5. *Ibid.*, p. 9.

6. *Ibid.*, p. 6.

7. *Ibid.*, p. 9.

8. The struggle for precision is at the heart of every effort at translation; unfortunately sometimes, in the effort, the language chosen creates new difficulties. At the risk of falling into the very error I've mentioned, I have used my own informal English version for the Italian passages rendered here.

9. For the Italian text, I have used C. H. Grandgent, ed., *La Divina Commedia* (Boston, New York, etc., D. C. Heath and Company, 1933), pp. 66-114.

10. The shepherd is the Pope, of course. The injunction in regard to clean and unclean beasts was familiar to the schoolmen. St. Augustine talks about the cloven hoof as symbolic of right conduct because it does not slip easily; and he interprets the chewing of the cud to signify wisdom.

11. Canto XXXIV, l. 25.

12. T. S. Eliot, 'Dante,' *Selected Essays*, 1917-1932 (New York, 1932), p. 212.

13. Canto XXXIV, l. 28.

14. Eliot, p. 212.

15. See: A. Bartlett Giammati, ed. *Dante in America: The First Two Centuries* (Medieval & Renaissance Texts & Studies, Binghamton, New York, 1983).

16. Shelley, *Selected Writings.*

17. T. S. Eliot, "A Talk on Dante," in *Dante in America: The First Two Centuries,* p, 219.

WOMEN IN THE POLITICAL LOVE-ETHIC OF THE *DIVINE COMEDY* AND THE *FAERIE QUEENE*

First published in Dante Studies, *XC, 1972.*
(For a major treatment of the women in the two epics see Anne Paolucci, *The Women in Dante's Divine Comedy and Spenser's Faerie Queene* (Griffon House Publications, 2005)

Dante's name is omitted from the cycle of epic poets reviewed by Spenser in his prefatory letter to Sir Walter Raleigh,[1] yet the poetic, moral, and political totality of the *Faerie Queene* suggests substantial parallels with the *Divine Comedy*. It is, in fact, the only major epic narrative in any modern language that invites serious comparison with Dante's great poem.[2]

One need not promote a tenuous thesis of conscious dependence or imitation to note significant similarities of design and theme in the two works. Spenser no less than Dante professed to having taken Virgil's *Aeneid* for a model. Like the *Aeneid*, the *Divine Comedy* and the *Faerie Queene* develop their epic themes around the twin foci of ethics and politics. For both poets the ethics is as much Aristotelian as it is Christian, and the politics is unmistakably imperial in the ancient Roman sense. On the other hand, Spenser's poetic habits are very different from Dante's (and this perhaps more than anything else has discouraged comparative analysis of the two poems). Although the ethical-political ends are very similar, Spenser moves poetically from symbol and type to historical reality, whereas Dante prefers to start with particularity, using recognizable individual characteristics to suggest universal types.[3] Even this difference, however, deserves to be explored carefully, for where Spenser and Dante depart from their usual methods the reversal points to similar motivations and underscores similar ideas.

What invites comparative study of the epic labors of Dante and Spenser most compellingly (one is tempted to say, with irresistible grace) is their poetic treatment of women. Spenser celebrates his living queen in her particular person and abstract glory as Dante celebrates his Beatrice and the Virgin Mary, and in this respect they have no peers in the long tradition of Western literature. In both poems, women are the source of misdirected action and the means of redemption; in both, women provide the initial thrust and inspiration and embody the final goal of the poetic adventure; in both, women are instrumental in integrating individual moral experience into the organic political whole. The carefully worked out progression toward the apex of meaning in which Gloriana and the Virgin Mary are revealed as first or final causes for the epic actions must convince us that the two poems were conceived with the same grand design and resemble one another in many and very basic ways.

As symbols of the , perfect political society, Gloriana and Mary remain — it is true — outside the troubled reality of everyday events. But they are also the summing up of history, and in that sense certainly are present throughout the action — particularly in the insistence on historical identification of figures (symbolic or real) and in teleological explanations. It is no accident that the large meanings of the poetic adventure, the epic nature and organic resolution of seemingly isolated events, are in both poems explained as visions accorded the women. Those events and the ethical and religious themes of the poems are evaluated and glossed in many different ways all along — and in this sense Marc Lombard, Farinata, Ugolino, Red Cross, Arthur, and Sansfoy (to name only a few of the memorable male figures of the two poems) are just as important as Francesca, Pia, Beatrice, Una, Duessa, and Britomart — but at the very top of the allegorical pyramid, where all meanings come together like meridians at the pole, women — not men — are singled out to provide the ultimate lesson. It is Britomart (guided by Alma) and Beatrice who at the key moment in the poems describe and comment on the course of human conduct as a meaningful progression toward an established end. The many episodes which furnish the ethical and political mosaic are shared — short of that ultimate lesson — by men and women equally; but in their special task of providing insight into the epic mission, in each case, certain women assume unique importance. It is toward this aspect of the discussion that our comments are directed. I would suggest that the historical chronicle reviewed in Alma's castle and the allegorical pageant at the top of Purgatorio provide the key parallel to be explored. In both, the all-important task of reviewing history within a providential design is reserved for the women. This alone justifies comparative analysis of the two poems in an organic and serious way; other parallels, though interesting in themselves, will be discussed only incidentally.

The significance and all-important role played by the women will not surprise us if we accept the premise that in both poems politics is conceived as a function of ethics. This may be clearer in Dante's case, but it is no less true of Spenser. The intention of both poets is to combine an individual odyssey — Mankind's quest for moral insight and personal salvation — with a political iliad — Mankind's struggle toward universal peace. Spenser's original plan, never fully realized, had been to depict the private or moral virtues in the first twelve books of the epic and the public virtues having to do with the establishment of government in the second twelve books. Dante's plan — fully and magnificently realized — was to depict simultaneously the regeneration of man and the realization of world peace. In both, love is the irresistible force which gives impetus and meaning to human conduct on all levels, and Woman the natural embodiment of that force. Within the framework of a love-ethic which is defined ultimately in political terms, Beatrice and the Virgin Mary, Britomart and Gloriana emerge as the most important voices of the two poems.

Dante's topographical structure enables him to integrate with the greatest economy the odyssey of the soul and the conflict which is the political iliad; the journey to personal salvation is also an exploration of the causes of the tragic struggle between the acknowledged spiritual and temporal heads of Christendom and a prophetic vision of God's providential resolution. Spenser's rich mosaic provides a complex network of inter-related allegorical incidents, each reinforcing singly and collectively the temptations in the way of the good life. In his wealth of incidents, Spenser approximates the reality of life more closely; Dante's method is to focus on the eternal moment where experience and insight merge — at once the clear statement and its unambiguous solution. Within these two schemes — only superficially or poetically different — the role of Woman emerges as the most important single element.

In the *Faerie Queene*, private and public virtues are illustrated in a series of interrelated episodes in which women are not — on the literal level, at least — consistently at the center of the action. Still, the total effect is not unlike that produced by Dante's tightly-knit scheme. Britomart, the champion of Chastity, is of course the central figure of Book III, and in the first book Una is almost as important as Red Cross; but the other female figures of the poem dominate isolated episodes in varying degrees, reinforcing the tension between good and evil in a variety of ways and settings. Amoret, Belphoebe, Florimell, Duessa, False Florimell, Malecasta, Lucifera, Hellenore, Una, Mirabella, Poeana, illustrate the positive and negative polarity of love in a series of variations at once the same and different. These many roles are interrelated by means of a cumulative series of experiences, each having its own spiritual tone and particular moral nuance. Thus the adventures of the two Florimells provide a kind of Augustinian lesson about evil as a deprivation of Good and therefore lacking substance; but this lesson strengthens in a number of ways the first and clearest opposition — that of Una and Duessa — in which selfish and altruistic love are drawn in stark contradiction. These and other pairs, in turn, provide rich poetic reverberations in the scattered adventures of such figures as Amoret, Lucifera,

Belphoebe, and the hags of the poem. Amoret perhaps comes closest to Dante's Francesca in the romantic vulnerability she reveals in the House of Busirane (and, I might add, in the romantic effect produced on the reader); but other figures such as Belphoebe and Florimell furnish related insights into the theme of misdirected or unsuspecting love. Mercilla, Irena, Belge, and Gloriana (together with the Faery Queen herself) embody the many aspects of the social and political message which Dante entrusts to the single figure of the inspired Beatrice. In her very personal role of spiritual counselor and guide, Una approximates the Beatrice of the last canto of Purgatorio. In her moving account of first causes, Mutabilitie has her counterpart in the Beatrice of the Paradiso.

Spenser, like Dante, makes much of the lure of beauty, weaving it directly or by implication into the larger ethical-political design. Acrasia attracts with her sensual appeal and gradually turns her lovers into beasts — a condition from which they can be saved only by outside intervention in the form of other powerful knights. False Florimell leads warriors astray by assuming the beautiful aspect of the true Florimell and destroys friendship and trust by arousing jealousy among her suitors. Duessa assumes the arresting shape and ways of Una to bring even the most virtuous knights to the brink of despair. Radigund's loveliness enslaves justice itself. Like Dante, Spenser reiterates the lesson that beauty without virtue is the instrument of destruction for the unsuspecting lover — just as virtuous beauty can be misinterpreted and arouse lust in the insensitive beholder. Even dreams are dangerous in this context: Archimago's spright disturbs Red Cross in his peaceful slumber, just as Dante's Siren bewitches and troubles the pilgrim-narrator as he sleeps on the mountain of Purgatory. Spenser's recurring types are ordered in the symphonic whole by juxtaposition, parallels, repetition, and transparent symbols; Dante's method is economical and direct. The Siren-Witch episode, for example, illuminates the Francesca episode with sharpness—

although it comes a whole *cantica* later. And that lesson is reviewed and analyzed fully, in the careful progression which is Dante's moral graph, at the top of *Purgatorio*, when regeneration is at hand and the pilgrim-narrator has been prepared for the final stage of personal purification. There Beatrice finally appears, assuming a combination of allegorical roles: the constant lover, the moral judge, the forgiving mistress, the spiritual counselor, the beautiful vision of the new life of love, the prophetic voice of salvation, the political historian, the grand teacher and explicator of allegory, the loving mother. Later, in the Paradiso, she becomes also the theologian of first causes. Dante's linear moral graph enables him to focus in Beatrice the full spectrum of literal, allegorical, moral, and anagogical roles which in Spenser are scattered in a rich profusion of female types, all of whom illustrate the polarity of love — the dramatic degeneration of personal virtue and political purpose on one hand, and the influx of courage and organic commitment to large ends on the other.

By virtue of a gracious command from on high, a command obeyed by Virgil in the best *stilnovist* tradition, Dante finally learns how he has been saved from a state not far removed from that of the victims of the Acrasias and Phaedrias of the *Faerie Queene*, to fulfill his role as political spokesman for the world that lives ill. That role hinges on his moral regeneration and is crowned with the promise of salvation. Like Red Cross — whose psychological and moral exhaustion also must be turned into new faith and courage in order for him to destroy the Dragon and reach Cleopolis — Dante learns the power of prayer in the drama of salvation. Beatrice's tearful exhortation forced Virgil out of Limbo to Dante's rescue at the beginning of the journey; her loving prayers all through the period of his straying were the assurance of his ultimate safety; Lucy's appeal and Mary's were the prayers that first brought Dante to the brink of remorse; and the exquisite tribute to Mary by St. Bernard is the ultimate reminder that prayer at its best is an inspired hymn of praise and thanksgiving. These moments of prayer constitute a progression toward insight — insight into both personal conduct and public duty.

Progression toward insight, through prayer, has its counterpart in Spenser's tale of Una and Red Cross. In the House of Busirane, Una prays Fidelia to instruct Red Cross; later, hearing of his sufferings and doubts, she appeals to Caelia for help; and in the prolonged battle with the Dragon, her steady prayers through two nights of uncertainty bring about miraculous recoveries in her knight, as often as he appears to have been overwhelmed by the beast. Spenser's characteristic moral dichotomy allows even for a kind of devil worship, as in Duessa's frustrated appeal to Night for help in her plan to destroy Red Cross. Here, as in Dante's account, the "conversion" from moral weakness to insight and regeneration is inextricably woven into the political theme: Dante must be "saved" in order to serve as the chosen vessel for Beatrice's message to the world; Red Cross must be finally redeemed before he can fight the Dragon that threatens Una and Cleopolis. In both, the power of prayer is dramatically embodied in the selfless love of women.

The value of prayer is indeed a major theme in both the first book of the *Faerie Queene* and in Purgatorio. In both, as we have seen, it is the women who are singled out as effective intermediaries. But beyond their roles as intermediaries and their important ministry as teachers of moral virtue, women serve in both epics as explicators of the grand design of history that governs the rise and fall of nations and empires. Alma and Britomart in Books II and III of the *Faerie Queene* make known the main lines of historical development that have led from ancient Troy, even as Beatrice, in the closing cantos of *Purgatorio*, provides Dante with a pageant-history of the two great institutions of Christendom — Holy Church and Holy Roman Empire — whose tragic conflict has made necessary the other-worldly journey of a new Aeneas, who must also be a new Paul. The central significance of the historical pageant of Purgatory is beyond question; and it is hardly an exaggeration to say, with Greenlaw, that in a

poem written as the *Faerie Queene* was, to celebrate the
ancestry of Elizabeth, the rhymed chronicles, "far from
being mere episodes . . . are important structurally."[4]
Greenlaw does not hesitate to say that Spenser's
"national feeling was closely connected with the idea of
the return of Arthur, and this is the organizing principle
of the great poem."[5]

There are, of course, fundamental differences in
the historical visions that sustain the epic movements of
the two poems. Historically, Spenser's purpose is the
patriotic glorification of an England ruled by the Tudors
as the seat of a world empire. Dante's purpose is
anything but "patriotic" in the nationalistic sense. The
empire he exalts is to be ruled by the German
Hohenstaufens — and he rages against the fragmented
powers of the Italian peninsula, both temporal and
spiritual, that have aspired and conspired to undermine
the temporal dominion of the Germanic emperors. Yes,
even this difference — sharp as it seems to be initially —
only serves to make the similarities in the two representations all the more striking.

Alma's castle is the well-governed soul, the
condition before the fall from grace — that same
condition which Dante regains at the top of Purgatory,
where, just before the appearance of Beatrice, Virgil
assures him he can proceed on his own initiative from
then on, since he soul is now master in its own house:

> Non aspettar mio dir più nè mio cenno;
>   libero, dritto e sano è tuo arbitrio,
>   e fallo fora non fare a suo senno:
> per ch'io te sovra te corono e mitrio.
>   (*Purg.* xxvii, 139-142)[6]

(Do not expect any more word or sign from me.
Your will is now free, upright, and whole;
and you would be at fault if you did not act
            according to its prompting;
therefore, I now crown and mitre you over yourself.)

In another important sense, Alma's castle may be said to
be the body politic in whose memory we read a chronicle
of Briton kings and Elfin emperors down to the time of

Gloriana — just as the mysterious Eden in which Dante finds himself prior to the appearance of Beatrice provides the background for the allegorical pageant which is the history of Mankind.

In both poems, the historical revelations are preceded by "self" revelations which bring self-knowledge; and these are directed in part or wholly by women. Arthur, in Canto IX of Book II, questions Praydesire about her sad and solemn aspect, only to be told that he is merely seeing himself reflected in her:

> Faire Sir (said she halfe in disdainfull wise)
> How is it, that this word in me ye blame,
> And in your selfe do not the same advise?
> Him ill beseemes, anothers fault to name,
> That may unwares be blotted with the same:
> Pensive I yield I am, and sad in mind,
> Through great desire of glory and of fame;
> Ne ought I weene are ye therein behind,
> That have twelve monthes sought one, yet no where
>   can her find.

(II, ix, 38)[7]

Guyon has a similar experience with Shamefastnesse — only, in this case, it is Alma who answers for the lady, saying, "She is the fountaine of your modestee" (43). Britomart, too, undergoes such an exposure in Book III, just before Merlin's prophecy to her. Her love for the knight she has seen in a vision is brought out into the open by Merlin and sanctioned by him as the will of providence (III, iii, 17-24). With Dante, the "self-revelation" is more in the form of an interruption, a deliberate casting aside of the "allegorical veil which, in the *Convivio*, he had attempted to throw over the things in the past. . . .[8] He has seen the approach of the heavenly lights (in the air, trailing color like brush strokes on canvas, and in the clear reflection of the water); he has heard the lovely melodies and harmonies that furnish the aural accompaniment for the almost unbearable impact of the scene; he has mourned the silent departure of Virgil and has turned like a fearful child to greet his lovely Beatrice. At this moment, the description of the allegorical pageant is interrupted and Beatrice reviews Dante's past life, preparing him for the passage across Lethe — the final purification, or rather, the clearing of the memory, before he views the historical spectacle. He is made to listen to his transgressions and to confess them openly; only after remorse and self-pity have thawed his heart and tears of repentance gush forth is he ready for the soothing balm of Lethe. He faints at the memory of his past sins and regains consciousness only in the water, with Matelda urging him to hold fast. Throughout the episode, other women join in — as Alma had answered for Shamefastnesse — to direct, encourage, and pity Dante. Dante's confession of remorse is the first step toward self-understanding and moral regeneration:

> Piangendo dissi: "Le presenti cose
>   col falso lor piacer volser miei passi,
>   tosto che 'l vostro viso si nascose."
>   (*Purg..* xxxi, 34-36)

> (I said, weeping: "The things around me,
> with their false pleasure, lured my steps away
> the minute your face was gone.")

In both poems, self-awareness is the prerequisite for the historical lessons, and these are marked by sharp stylistic changes which isolate the passages and give them special significance. Spenser's historical chronicle is a literal account framed in a carefully worked-out allegory; Dante's historical pageant is an allegorical masque — a departure from Dante's usual descriptive realism. Both passages end abruptly: Dante is left wondering, when the great car which is the center of interest in the masque is suddenly drawn out of sight into the woods. Arthur is interrupted by missing pages in the manuscript. Both representations have dramatic moments in which exclamations shock the concentrated visual attention and provide a literal gloss. Arthur reads at a certain moment in the chronicle: "But O, the greedy thirst of royall crowne,/That knowes no kinred, nore regards no right . . .."; Dante hears a voice cry out:

> O navicella mia, come mal se' carca!
>   (*Purg.* xxxi, 129)

(O my little bark, how you are weighted down!)

At the heart of both episodes is a teleological conception of history, which in its optimistic tone and in its effort to combine history and myth furnishes the reader with the key to meaning. Having read the chronicle of British kings, Arthur is "quite ravisht with delight" and is inspired to cry out:

> . . . Deare countrey, O how dearely deare
> Ought thy remembraunce, and perpetuall band
> Be to thy foster Childe, that from thy hand
> Did commun breath and nouriture receave?
> How brutish is it not to understand,
> How much to her we owe, that all us gave,
> That gave unto us all, what ever good we have.
>
> (II, x, 69)

Dante too is ravished with the vision he sees; again and again he reminds us of the difficulty of describing adequately what he sees and resorts to analogies and similes. The profusion of imagery here is a reminder of the double transcendence of the opening canto of Inferno and the vision of God at the end of the poem. The episode is singled out in this way as the third important "key" passage of the poem. He too, like Arthur, lashes out against the corruption that has taken place in the world. The very description of the car and the creatures that take part in the masque is charged with meaning: the swooping down of the eagle and the rending of the car, the fox "che d'ogni pasto buon parca digiuna" (*Purg.* xxxii, 120), Beatrice's rebuke to the beast, the dragon who further damages the car with its "coda maligna" (134), the shameless harlot "con le ciglie pronte" (150), the giant fondling her, his jealous rage against the "puttana" (160) who turns her attention elsewhere. The reader of the chronicle and Dante the spectator-narrator are emotionally and intellectually involved; both are aware of the corruption around them, but at the same time both are aware of the promise of a providential resolution.

The two episodes bring together the wide sweep

of history and the wealth of myth into an organic picture of reality. Spenser's description of the destruction of the original monstrous inhabitants of the land by Brutus, the subsequent unification of the various regions, the rivalries and wars, the new strain derived from Numa the lawgiver, the struggle with the Romans, the succeeding generations of rulers and the wars of usurpation, the coming of the Saxons, the restoration of constituted authority — the whole inventory of claims, counterclaims, battles, intrigues, invasions — all tend toward a providential end which is the divine and glorious right of the English nation, under the rule of the successors of King Arthur, to world domination, a right made clear in Merlin's prophecy to Britomart, in which the thread of the narrative is picked up at about the time that Alma's chronicle breaks off and is continued into more recent times. Guyon's reading of the history of Faery Land — seemingly independent of Arthur's — reinforces the idea of destiny in English history by tracing Gloriana's line back to Prometheus and Elfe (Man) and connecting the Faery Queen with a vision seen by Arthur — a vision with which he falls in love. Both Arthur and Guyon are moved by the historical review of the shaping of the national center of a great empire, whose destiny is guided by divine providence and whose greatest moment is yet to come. Gloriana, as the Faery Queen, embodies the realization of that grand imperial design, to which Arthur had given spontaneous profession of love and loyalty. Her unseen influence motivates the adventures of the virtuous knights of the poem — Red Cross's destruction of the Dragon, Guyon's capture of the enchantress Acrasia, Artegall's redress of Irena's wrongs — but it is particularly felt in Book III, where Gloriana's presence is forever before us in Belphoebe's dedication to chastity and Britomart's noble enterprise: a beautiful complementary portrait of the actual Queen.

The vision of nationalistic British imperialism — an imperialism in which the enforceable world peace of the Roman imperial system so dear to Dante is replaced by a more easily enforceable balance of power system, designed to relieve the "happy few" of their warden-like responsibilities while enabling them to prosper industrially and commercially in the freedom of their island kingdom — gives way ultimately before the might of Mutabilitie and Nature. The vision of Cleopolis, the most magnificent of earthly cities, gives way to the vision of the eternal heavenly city, a change already announced in Book I:

> Till now, and then the knight, I weened well,
> That great Cleopolis, where I have beene,
> In which the fairest Faerie Queene doth dwell,
> That fairest Citie was, that might be seene;
> And that bright towre all built of christall cleene,
> Panthea, seemed the brightest thing, that was:
> But now by proofe all otherwise I weene;
> For this great Citie that does far surpas,
> And this bright Angels towre quite dims that towre of glas.
> (I, x, 59)

The promise of Cleopolis is surpassed by the promise of the heavenly City; and in the light of that promise, the existential pessimism of the Mutabilitie cantos must be read as the necessary but temporary reversal in the dialectic which leads to ultimate happiness. The Mutabilitie cantos, it must be remembered, are fragmentary; they end the poem, as it has come down to us, but they are not the final statement in the organic progression Spenser had in mind. The negative thrust of the Mutabilitie cantos reflects Spenser's characteristic dichotomy: the forces of good are constantly at war with the forces of evil; and although the outcome is not always a complete triumph of good, the sides are never confounded.

In Dante's scheme, on the contrary, the central conflict involves the opposition of two supreme goods of man. The pageant that he sees (which justifies his having taken the long journey through Hell and Purgatory) is a grand survey of the relations of the two chief institutions of Christendom, Holy Roman Empire and Holy Roman Church, from the time of Christ's coming into the world to the so-called Babylonian captivity of the Papacy in the fourteenth century. In it we see the history of a tremendous struggle, beginning with glad tidings of great joy for all mankind, and ending, or apparently ending, in complete disaster. In the course of the strange masque, Dante witnesses a series of dramatic incidents or confrontations, all of which have to do with the power struggle between Church and State. There can be no doubt as to the function of this episode. Here for the first time Dante is given a straightforward answer (but not yet the final one) as to why he has come on this journey — the question posed to Virgil in the opening cantos is taken up by Beatrice, who instructs Dante to watch closely and report what he sees to the rest of the world on his return.

What he sees sums up, in fact, the whole of human experience, identifying it with the two strains of temporal and spiritual activity — and these are resolved into the single history of imperial rule as guardian of the true Church in the world. As in the histories of Arthur, Guyon, Britomart, and Paridell, the seeming complexities and accidents of the past are interpreted according to a purpose which is above individual intentions and human actions. In both representations, there is a strong suggestion of a heteronomy of divine ends, realized through the autonomy of men.

Dante's historical summary depicts the tragic reality of the shattering confrontation of the Church and the Empire — the two institutions provided by God for men on earth. The symbolic pageant reviews the coming of Christ into the world, the damage wreaked by the donation of Constantine, the temporal ambitions of the Church, the fragmentation brought on by heresies, and the corruption of the Papacy in his time, when the lure of temporal supremacy was greatest. Here, as in Spenser's account, the pessimism of the historical actuality is relieved by a promise of good to come:

Da tema e da vergogna
  voglio che tu omai ti disviluppe,
   sì che non parli più com' om che sogna.
Sappi che 'l vaso che 'l serpente ruppe,
  fu e non è; ma chi n' ha colpa, creda
  che vendetta di Dio non teme suppe.

Non sará tanto tempo sanza reda
  l'aquila che lasciò le penne at carro,
  per che divenne mostro e poscia preda. . . .
              (*Purg.*. xxxiii, 31-39)

(I want you now to free yourself
  of all traces of fear and shame.
  so that you no longer speak like a man dreaming.
I want you to know that the vessel the serpent broke,
  was but is no more; but let the guilty one believe
  that God's vengeance fears no sops.
The eagle that left its plumage on the car,
  transforming it into a monster and then prey
  Will not be long without an heir. . . .)

    Beatrice's historical summary — in which the pessimism of temporal reality is balanced by the optimism of divine resolution — provides, like the summaries offered by Alma, a new impetus for the epic journey. That journey ends, for Dante, in the vision of God, where the tragic spectacle of the world is reduced to insignificance. For Spenser, the dream of world dominion ends in the vision of Mutalibilite — that stoic divinity so like the winged woman, Albrecht Dürer"s Melencolia, who surveys the world of change with the sadness of truth, which is insight into necessity. The grand procession of Seasons, Months, Day and Night, Life and Death is not so different from Dante's journey through the heavens in search of ultimate explanations. Beatrice enlightens Dante; Mutabilitie is silenced but not repudiated in the verdict of Nature. The ideas of fixed purpose and change are reconciled, for Spenser, on a higher level which remains implicit — just as the scattered events of history are reduced to proper perspective in Dante's last vision of God.

    The pessimism of Spenser's Mutabilitie is the pessimism of all temporal things in a divine universe whose promised fulfillment lies outside itself,

          . . . Eternity,
That is còntrary to Mutabilitie.
        (VI, viii, 2)

That pessimism is discernible in Dante's nostalgic reminder of what was lost with the death of Henry VII:

E 'n quel gran seggio a che tu li occhi tieni
   per la corona che giù v'è su posta,
   prima che tu a queste nozze ceni,
sederà l'alma, che fia giù agosta,
   dell'alto Arrigo, ch' a drizzar Italia
   verrà in prima ch' ella sia disposta.
            (*Purg.*. xxxiii, 31-39)

(On that throne on which your eyes are riveted
   because of the crown set above it,
   even before you join this wedding feast,
the soul of the mighty Henry shall be seated,
   he who shall come to raise Italy
   long before she is ready for it.)

In the very next canto, the temporal is contrasted with the eternal in a magnificent political conception with which Dante expresses his wonder at the point he has reached in his journey:

Se i barbari, venendo da tal plaga
   che ciascun giorno d'Elice si cuopra,
   rotante col suo figlio ond' ella è vaga,
veggendo Roma e l' ardua sua opra,
   stupefaciensi, quando Laterano
   a le cose mortali andò di sopra;
io, che al divino da l'umano,
   a l'etterno dal tempo era venuto,
   e di Fiorenza in popol giusto e sano,
di che stupor dovea esser compiuto!
            (*Par.* xxxi, 31-40)

(If the Barbarians coming from such a region
   as that which every day is spanned by Helice,
   who turns with her son for whom she yearns,
were stupified at the sight of Rome
   and her mighty works at that time, when Lateran
   rose high above mortal things;
imagine the stupor that overwhelmed me,
   coming as I had from the human to the divine,
   from time to eternity, from Florence to a wholesome
            and just people!)

What Dante gives us in these vivid contrasts is the resolution of Mutabilitie. It has been suggested that after completing the first three books of his epic, Spenser revised his scheme so as to introduce in the fifth book the matter originally intended for the second cycle of twelve books. If we accept this theory, then Spenser's boast that he has been steadfast in his ultimate object assumes new importance. Tillyard has observed that the whole question of the arrangement of parts in the *Faerie Queene* is still open to discussion, and he suggests that Spenser working with "a kind of unconscious tact" realized at some point in the composition of the poem that the original plan could not work, that "one allegorical quality was apt to impinge on another and that he was making his ethical scheme too political to allow, without redundance, his proposed sequel. . . ." [9] This view is reinforced by Spenser's reminder, in the last canto of Book VI, that he has been steadfast in his purpose.

> Like a ship, that through the ocean wyde
> Directs her course unto one certaine cost,
> Is met of many a counter winde and tyde,
> With which her winged speed is let and crost,
> And she her selfe in stormie surges tost;
> Yet making many a borde, and many a bay,
> Still winneth way, ne hath her compasse lost:
> Right so it fares with me in this long way.
> Whose course is often stayd, yet never is astray.
>
> (VI, xii, 1)

He was, we may assume, approaching the kind of poetic vision that Dante had, in which the moral odyssey was intimately woven with the political iliad — and history, embodied in the figure of Mutablitie, was to give way ultimately to the glorious eternal contemplation of God.

Whatever the structure and design of the *Faerie Queene*, there can be no doubt that Spenser exalted Woman as the unique prophet of eternal happiness. Like Dante, he saw in her the principle of knowledge, insight, and the inspiration to moral and political action through love. In their pursuit of peace, the partisan of a proud and prosperous England and the ardent propagandist of universal empire begin by paying homage to the arresting power of beauty; both follow — according to a tradition of poetic inspiration at least as old as Plato — the impulse of love to its ulimate end, where all differences are confounded and the *many* gathered into the *one*, like the scattered pages of nature's multiplicity (as Dante says) marvelously bound by love, in a single volume:

> . . . vedi che s'interna,
>   legato con amore in un volume,
>   ciò che per l'universo si squaderna.
>   (*Par.* xxxiii, 85-87)

> (. . . I saw gathered together,
>   bound by love in one volume,
>   that which in the universe is scattered.)

NOTES

1. It is worth noting that Spenser's prefatory letter introduces a dream or vision similar to that recorded by Dante at the close of the *Vita Nuova*. Arthur, the hero of the *Faerie Queene*, is inspired by the dream to seek "the Faery Queen, with whose excellent beauty ravished, he awaking resolved to seeke her out, and so . . . went to seeke her forth in Faery Land." (*The Works of Edmund Spenser, A Variorum Edition*, ed. Edwin Greenlaw, Charles Grosvenor Osgood, Frederick Morgan Padelford, Ray Heffner, and others, 11 vols. [Baltimore: Johns Hopkins Press, 1932-57], vol. I, p. 168.) Dante had written:

> apparve a me una mirabile visione, ne la quale io vidi cose che mi fecero proporre di non dire più di questa benedetta infino a tanto che io potesse più degnamente trattare di lei. . . . E poi piaccia a colui che è sire de la cortesia, che la mia anima se ne possa gire a vedere la gloria de la sua donna, cioè di quella benedetta Beatrice, la quale gloriosamente mira ne la faccia de colui *qui est per omnia secula benedictus*. (*Le Opere di Dante. Testo Critico della Società Dantesca Italiana*, a cura di Michele Barbi, et. al. [Firenze: Bemporad, 1921], p. 53.)

2. James Russell Lowell marvelled, in 1876, that "none of the commentaries on Spenser notice his most important obligations" to Dante ("Spenser," *Among My Books*, Second Series [Boston: Houghton, Mifflin, 1897], first printed, 1876, p. 182, n.). More recently, Leicester Bradner, Harry Berger, Jr., and A. C. Hamilton have noted specific (but isolated) parallels and similarities. Hamilton stresses the fact that "both poems share a similar critical history" and concludes that "Spenser criticism needs to catch up." (*The Structure of Allegory in 'The Faerie Queene'* [Oxford: Clarendon Press, 1961], pp. 30-33.) See also: Henry J. Todd, ed. *The Works of Edmund Spenser* (London, 1805, n, pp. 18ff.; E. H. Plumptre, trans. *The Commedia and the Canzoniere of Dante Alighieri* (London: Isbister, 1887), Vol. II, pp. 227, 358, 428, 429; Emil Koppel, "Dante in der Englischen Litt. Des 16 Jahrh.,"

in Zeitschrift für vergleichende Literaturgeschichte, III (1890), 449-451; Don Cameron Allen, *Image and Meaning: Metaphoric Traditions in Renaissance Poetry* (Baltimore: Johns Hopkins Press, 1960), p. 31; Ida Langdon, *Materials for a Study of Spenser's Theory of Fine Art* (Ithaca, New York: Cornell University Press, 1911), pp. xlii-xliv; Michele Renzulli, *Dante nella letteratura inglese* (Firenze: "La Via," 1926), p. 40; Alfred Satterthwaite, *Spenser, Ronsard, and Du Bellay* (Princeton, New Jersey: Princeton University Press, 1960), p. 208; John Arthos, *On the Poetry of Spenser and the Form of Romances* (London: Allen and Unwin, 1965), p. 50; and Josephine Waters Bennett, "Genre, Milieu, and the 'Epic-Romance'," in *English Institute Essays*, 1931, ed. Alan S. Downer (New York: Columbia University Press, 1952), p. 125.

3. A careful analysis of the method of the two poems is long overdue. It might serve, among other things, to put to rest the notion that Dante must be thoroughly "explained" allegorically in order to be appreciated and — by the same token — the notion that Spenser's allegory is "old-fashioned." The truth is that Dante is as modern in his forthright and dramatic realism as Spenser is in his surrealistic manner of description.

4. *The Works of Edmund Spenser, a variorum Edition*, ed. Edwin Greenlaw, etc., Vol. II, p. 453.

5. *Ibid.*, p. 493.

6. *Le Opere di Dante, Testo Critico della Società Dantesca Italiana*, a cura di Michele Barbi, et. al. (English versions of quotations from the *Commedia* are my own.)

7. Quotations from Spenser are from the *Variorum* edition and will be identified in the text.

8. Edmund Gardner, *Dante* (London: J.M. Dent, 1923) p, 148.

9. E.M.W. Tillyard, *The English Epic and its Background* (New York: Oxford University Press, 1954), pp. 286-287.

EXILE AMONG EXILES:
DANTE'S PARTY OF ONE

First published in Mosaic, *VIII/3*
(University of Manitobia Press), 1975

Exile is the all-pervasive state of mind of the *Divine Comedy*. Everywhere he goes, through the low, middle, and high regions of the dead, Dante comes upon Florentines who remind him of home, and his talk with them, even in the highest reaches of Paradiso, is invariably the talk of an exile.

In Dante's Christian universe, all of human life on earth is, of course, a journey in exile. This soul that rises with us, our life's star, is created by God Himself, and there is no rest for it therefore until it rests in Him. It is in the middle of his life's journey on earth that Dante finds himself singled out providentially to take "another journey" (*un altro viaggio*)[1] which will provide, in its poetic narration, a new Holy Writ for mankind: a sacred poem (*poema sacro*)[2] which by God's grace will have in its beauty a power "to remove those living in this life from a state of misery and to lead them to a state of happiness."[3]

For the damned souls in Dante's Hell, man's temporary exile from God on earth becomes an everlasting exile. The sum and substance of that Hell is an exile's endlessly frustrated longing for the light and love of God. "We live in desire," says Virgil, speaking for all his honored pagan colleagues suspended gracelessly on the edge of Hell, "without hope" (*senza speme*).[4] That is the least common denominator — the bottom line, so to speak — of Hell's anguish. The anguish mounts with each downward turn of the spiral until we reach the frozen wastes of Cocytus, at the point in the universe most distant from God, where Lucifer, originally Heaven's brightest and liveliest intelligence, numbly endures his everlasting banishment.

Except for the grace of the Crucifixion on Golgotha, every man, woman, and child ever born would have passed out of this life into Hell's everlasting exile. All who share, through baptism, in the death of that Crucifixion, can share also in its promise of an exile's eventual return to God. Baptism is a way through Hell to Heaven, but it is not an infallible way. The trials of life — its spotted leopards, lions, and she-wolves — can bar its course, undo its promise. That is Dante's condition at the beginning of the *Divine Comedy*. He has been baptized in Florence half a life-time ago, in the font of his beautiful St. John's (*nel mio bel San Giovanni*).[5] But now, for a variety of reasons, he finds himself separated from that font, both physically and spiritually: physically, because his political enemies have banished him from Florence; spiritually, because he has failed to live up to its sacramental promise. Political and spiritual exile converge in that mid-point of Dante's life, where, with a sudden, almost Pentecostal, gift of words dictated by love in his heart, he presumed not only to vie with Homer and Virgil as an epic poet but even, and quite literally, to "write like God" for mankind's spiritual salvation.[6]

In the early years of political exile from his native Florence, Dante no doubt hoped and planned, with other exiled partisans, to make a speedy return by forcible means. He had left Florence as a member of an embassy to Rome, sent by the Council of the Hundred to protest the Pope's policy, which favored a rival faction against the governing party. While there, his party lost control of the government at home, and the new regime (according to a practice almost universal in the experience of popular government) sought at once to strengthen itself by "impeaching" and ousting its old rivals from whatever positions of power they had retained. Dante was charged with "barratry" — with using his office to extort money and make illicit profits by other means. A fine was imposed. And as Dante did not return to pay it, he was subsequently sentenced to two years' banishment. The penalties mounted with his continued refusal to submit himself to the authorities, until finally he and several other, now guilty of *lese majesty*, were condemned to be buried alive if ever they fell "into the hands of the Commonwealth."[7]

In the early pages of his *Symposium* or *Banquet* (*Convivio*), Dante tells us of the bitterness of his exile:

> Alas, would it had pleased the Dispenser of the Universe that I should never have had to make excuses for myself; that neither others had sinned against me, nor I had suffered this punishment unjustly, the punishment I say of exile and poverty! Since it was the pleasure of the citizens of the fairest and most renowned daughter of Rome, Florence, to cast me out from her most sweet bosom (wherein I was born and brought up to the climax of my life, and wherein I long with all my heart, and with their good leave, to repose my wearied spirit, and to end the days allotted me), wandering as a stranger through almost every region to which our language reaches, I have gone about as a beggar, showing against my will the wound of fortune, which is often wont to be imputed unjustly to the fault of him who is stricken. Verily, I have been a ship without sails and without rudder, driven to various harbours and shores by the parching wind which blows from pinching poverty. And I have appeared vile in the eyes of many, who, perhaps from some aspect of me, had imagined me in a different guise.[8]

Modern commentators have inevitably drawn comparisons between Dante's lot and that of modern political exiles. "It is more difficult," writes the Swedish journalist-critic Olof Lagercrantz, "for the modern exile." In Dante's time, he notes, there was a common language, Latin, spoken by all men of culture, and a common faith, Christianity, which manifested itself pretty much the same everywhere. That basic fellowship of values made it possible, it would seem, for an exile of Dante's time to find friends and companions almost anywhere. Lagercrantz cites as a modern contrast the case of Trotsky who, "cast out of the communist fellowship but retaining his communist convictions, became in the West — which saw in him a bloodstained hangman — a wandering Jew, a beggar, an outlaw driven from door to door, who was finally struck down by his mighty rival's revenge and died from wounds inflected by an ice pick. But," he concludes, "Dante was little better off. Like Trostky, one of his severest torments was that he was vilified in his own country and everything he had done was distorted and misconstrued, while none could or would defend him."[9]

G. A. Borgese, himself a modern exile driven out of Italy by the fascist government, holds — on the contrary — that exile in Dante's time was apt to have far worse consequences than today. "No modern exile," Borgese wrote in *Goliath* (1937),

> can measure the anguish of the medieval expatriate. The medieval city, loud and fierce as a bee-hive, had developed in the narrow interplay of its actions and passions a system of psychic self-sufficiency which approaches the completeness of an animal instinct. The bee-hive, for all its cruelty, is the only possibility of life for the single bee; so was a medieval society like the Italian commune to its children. Expulsion was a curse. Exile was agony.[10]

The great poetic paradox of the *Divine Comedy* — read as an exile's epic journey back to God — is that, the closer its Christian hero gets to God, the more poignant is his expression of anguish as a Florentine expatriate. Among the damned souls in Hell, he is full of defiance still. In the 10th Canto of *Inferno* he depicts for us the stupendous figure of Farinata degli Uberti, free-thinking materialist, honored by all as the "savior of Florence"[11] because, when his own partisans in exile had it within their power to raze the city to the ground, and had voted to do so, he had stood alone against their determined will and had prevailed. Part of the condition of souls in Hell is that, while they know in advance events yet to come on earth, they are blind to present happenings. And so, when Dante confronts them, there is usually an exchange of current news for prophecy. Dante dated his epic journey beyond the grave as occurring in late March 1300, when his exile is still in the future, and when the news he brings from Florence is painful indeed for the great partisan Farinata.

Farinata burns in Hell for having insisted willfully that the human soul dies with the body — a view by no means rare in Dante's Florence. His place of everlasting exile from God is a spacious plain that

reminds Dante of the Roman cemetery at Arles. He walks
with Virgil among the high stone tombs of the necropolis,
each with its lid open and glowing hot, like a furnace,
with flames licking out incessantly. Out of one of the fiery
tombs, a voice cries out to him:

> O Tuscan who walks living through the fire
> of our grim city, uttering honest speech,
> pause, if it please you, briefly where you stand.
> Your language to my ear proclaims you one
> born in that noble fatherland which I
> perhaps too harshly dealt with.
> (*Inf.* x. 22-27)[12]

Dante, caught unawares by the voice, turns about as if in
fear, and is chided by his guide Virgil. Farinata has risen
in his tomb, emerging head and breast above the fire. He
stood, says Dante, with

> . . . chest out-thrust and haughty-browed
> as if all Hell he held in vast contempt.
> (*Inf.* x. 35-36)

Dante is warned by Virgil to measure his words; yet
before he can utter a single one, Farinata asks him
almost angrily: "Who were your elders?" Dante hastens to
tell, and that precipitates a marvelously brief dramatic
dialogue, the full force of which can hardly be sensed
before Farinata lapses into an agonized silence. Upon
learning the identity of Dante's family, Farinata says:

> Sworn enemies they were to me and mine
> and to my party, twice I drove them forth
> (*Inf.* x. 46-48)

— to which Dante, with knowledge of present things
unknown to Farinata, quickly retorts:

> If twice thrust out, yet twice they made return,
> An art your partisans have yet to learn.
> (*Inf.* x. 49-51)

These words stun Farinata into silence. And while he
broods, Dante carries on a brief, poignant exchange with
Cavalcanti — father of Dante's friend and fellow-poet —
who, like Farinata, is damned to the living death of the
Epicurean materialists. This tender nostalgic encounter
— in which Cavalcanti, having recognized Dante, asks
why Guido is not there with him — is a masterpiece in

contrapuntal effects. When Cavalcanti, misinterpreting
Dante's words to mean that his son Guido is dead, drops
out of sight, Farinata resumes where he left off.

> . . . But that great-hearted one at whose behest
> I had first stopped had altered not his mien,
> not even so much as moved his neck or side,
> but spoke in sharp rebuttal to my thrust:
> "If my folk leave that lesson still unlearned
> it more torments me than this bed of mine."

Hell has no agonies to compare with the exiled patriot's
agony on earth. And Dante, Farinata warns, will soon
have his taste of it:

> "How bitter is the schooling in that skill
> you too will know, yea, even before the queen
> here regnant fifty times renew her glow.
> But as you cherish hope to see again
> the fair earth overhead, disclose to me
> why such remorseless foes to all my kin
> your people show themselves in every law."
> "The slaughter and the carnage," I replied.
> "that colored Arbia's waters with our blood
> calls forth such vengeful prayers at our shrines."
> Sighing he shook his head and made reply:
> "Not I alone and not without just cause
> had hand in that, but I alone stood forth
> defending Florence when the cry went out
> to raze her walls and blot her from the earth."
>
> (*Inf.* x. 73-93)

Despite the partisan fury of Dante's party
against him, Farinata is honored in his exile, even
beyond the grave. He had dealt perhaps too harshly, as
he himself acknowledges, with his beloved Florence when
his enemies governed it. The blood ran thick, perhaps too
much of it. But he was not alone in the heat of battle;
and his cause, he insists, was just — proof of which is the
fact that he, acting alone, saved the city from total
destruction in its darkest hour.

Dante's exile will be far more painful, with little
scope for partisan pride. He will long to revenge himself
upon his enemies who drive him out; but, tragically, he
will come to hate and eventually to despise his fellow
exiles even more. It is from the soul of one of those
"elders" about whom Farinata had inquired that Dante

will "learn" the details of the hard lessons of exile he would soon have to face, according to Farinata's prophecy. In Canto XVII of Paradiso, Dante's great great grandfather Cacciaguida, who had fought and died for the faith in the Crusades, is asked directly by our pilgrim-hero to tell "what sort of fortune lies in store" for him, so that he may expect, if not avoid, the worst. "There comes upon my vision," says Cacciaguida —

> . . . your approaching time.
> As through his cruel and faithless stepmother
> Hippolytus was expelled from Athens, so
> you from your Florence will be forced to flee.
> This is now willed, indeed already planned
> and shortly will be done by one who schemes
> there where all day Christ is put up for sale.
> The blame will follow the offended side
> in rumor, as is wont, but vengeance yet
> by truth dispensed shall witness to the truth.
> You will abandon everything you love
> most dearly, this is but the arrow first
> discharged by exile's bow; thereafter too
> you shall learn how salty to the taste
> is alien bread, and come to feel how hard
> another's stairs are to descend and mount.
> And what shall heaviest weigh your shoulders down
> will be the company of fools and rogues
> with which you shall fall down into this vale,
> for ingrates all, and impious and mad
> they'll turn on you; but in short course of time
> they and not you will bear the temples red.
> So that it will redound to your fair fame
> that you have made a party for yourself.
>   (*Par.* xvii. 44-69)

Dante in exile is thus destined to become an exile among the exiled. Deeming his partisans fools and rogues and ingrates — impious and mad — he will constitute himself a party of one against them all and count upon the high inspiration of his poetry, rather than upon their partisan stratagems, to overcome the cruelty of his banishment.

The 19th century poet, James Thomson, whose *City of Dreadful Night* is the closest thing to Dantesque poetry in English (but who could also write venemous satire worthy of Swift), knew well from his own experience in social exile among the atheist-republicans of Charles Bradlaugh's *National Reformer*, what prompted Dante to make a party for himself. In one of his most brilliant satires, "Proposals for the Speedy Extinction of Evil and Misery," which is alternately Rabelesian and Swiftian in its humor, Thomson proposes that mankind, as the manifest crown and head, as the supreme intelligence of a godless universe, could easily make a speedy extinction of evil and misery by threatening a universal strike against the whole progressive, evolutionary business. "This is the forcible plan of strikes by labor against capital," Thomas writes, "applied in its utmost extension by man against nature; as you have already mere trades' unions, organize a universal Man-union, and threaten, if all your demands are not immediately granted, to 'strike' living, to 'turn out' of human existence, and you will at once bring the everlasting employer to reason. . . . Here is the dreadful *ultimatum*: Immediate compliance with all we ask (which we ask for your good no less than for our own), or we immediately kill ourselves, thus beheading you.[13]

But what if, among the malcontent "reformers" of 19th-century England, no one will take this initiative? He, at least, will not have to bear responsibility for the consequent damnation of Man and Nature; like Dante, he will be an exile among the exiled:

> I can wash the hands of brave endeavor in the water of absolution, and smoke the pipe of tranquility on the cushion of good conscience: for as our brave German kinsmen say (especially when, after beating the enemy, they have requisitioned a jolly dinner and are billeted to a luxurious bed), A good conscience is a soft pillow — *Ein gutes Gewissen ist ein sanftes Kissen*. And remaining thus in a sublime minority of one (as remaineth eternally the most dread Lord God of monotheism), I can administer unto myself the consolation of that blessed truth that Cacciaguida in Paradise administered to Dante (the Dante Durante, the long-enduring Giver), the supreme stoical truth for the honest and independent thinker: Well shall it be for thee, to have made thyself a party by thyself: *Sì ch' a te fia bello averti fatta parte per te stesso*.[14]

Dante, the political exile, knows that he is no

Farinata. He has been swept up by the politics of his time, and he has proposed — as poets usually do — his far-fetched and self-righteous "final solution." Yet he knows his true worth as a poet and prophesies his everlasting fame. In the end he knows that he has been sent into exile so that he might write his great Christian epic of an exile's return, not to Florence, in the train of a conquering emperor, but to God. He has been driven out of his native Florence, where he was twice born — once in nature, in his mother's womb, and once again in grace, through baptism in Christ's death and the promise of His resurrection. Recalling his baptism "nel mio bel San Giovanni" he gives expression to the exile's deepest nostalgia and loving desire. One way or another he will return to Florence. It will come to pass, it *must* come to pass, because of the power of his poetry, because of the *Commedia*, where he has pursued the course of beauty like an arrow straight up to God, as no human poet had ever done before.

Early in *Paradiso*, absolutely confident of his poetic powers, he warns readers not to try to follow him further, unless they come with a long training and discipline in high philosophy:

> O ye who in your little bark have come,
> after my ship that cuts the waves with song,
> eager to hear, O turn ye back again
> to look on your own shores, nay set not forth
> on that wide Ocean sea, lest it may hap
> that, losing sight of me, ye go astray.
> The sea I range was never coursed before:
> Minerva blows, Apollo guides me on
> and the nine Muses point me out the Bears.
> (*Par.* ii, 1-9)

Under the highest form of poetic imagination, Dante tells us (with the arrogance of genius), he is presuming to take up a subject so transcendent that no other earthly poet — not Homer, not Virgil — had dared to make it his theme. The Jews of the Old Testament and the Christians of the New Testament know the kind of experience he is contemplating; but they were convinced that it transcended human art. Who can follow his poetry on such high seas?

Ye other few who at the proper season
raised up your necks toward the angelic bread
which surfeits none while it sustains life here,
you may indeed upon the salty deep
entrust your ship and follow on my furrow
before the waves that fall back unevenly.

(Par. ii, 10-15)

In Paradiso we are to witness the highest
religious and philosophic experience transformed into
the subject-matter of poetry; no one has ever before
attempted it. It is a spiritual prolongation of Dante's
political exile. To that end he was made to suffer
banishment upon banishment, as an exile among the
exiled. Such is the lesson of Cacciaguida's prophecy. He
must make his way alone, finally, to the unexplored
heights. Yet, even when he has scaled those heights and
seen it all — the scattered pages of the universe bound
together, as he says, by love in a single volume — he
makes this pathetically sad, sublimely beautiful, self-
confident exile's prophecy:

If ever it should come to pass that the sacred
poem, in which both heaven and earth have had
a hand, making me lean over the years,
succeed in overwhelming the cruelty that keeps me
locked outside the lovely sheepfold, where I
slept a lamb — the enemy of wolves who harrass it —
then with a new voice and fleece I shall return
as Poet, and at my baptismal font
accept the laurel crown;
for it was there I entered in that faith
which makes souls known to God, and for its sake
Peter, later, circled thus my brow.[15]

Il poema sacro al quale ha posto mano e cielo e terra: in
that deceptively simple phrase, Dante sums up his daring
ars poetica. With earthly, pagan skill guided by Virgil, but
also with divine inspiration, he has given us a masterful
expression of art on the verge of transcending itself. This
alone serves to make the *Divine Comedy* sublimely
unique. Dante is the first poet of the West, and perhaps
the last, to recognize the absolute limits of art and to
attempt the inexpressible in art, right up to the highest
source of his inspiration — which is the blinding light of

divine love that graciously compels the faithful exile home.

NOTES

1. Inferno, ii, 91.

2. Paradiso, xxv, 1

3. Letter to Can Grande della Scala," in *Literary Criticism: Plato to Dryden*, ed. Allan H. Gilbert (Detroit, 1962), p. 205.

4. Inferno, iii, 42..

5. Inferno, xix, 17.

6. See: Olof Lagercrantz, *From Hell to Paradise* (New York, 1966), pp. 86ff.

7. See Paget Toynbee, *Dante Alighieri* (New York, 1965), p. 84.

8. *Convivio*, I, iii, 3-6. Cited by Toynbee, p. 89.

9. Lagercrantz, p. 119.

10. Cited by Thomas G. Bergin in *Dante* (Boston, 1965), p. 28.
11. See Paget Toynbee, *Concise Dante Dictionary* (Oxford, 1914), p. 221.

12. Unless otherwise indicated, translations cited are from Thomas G. Bergin, *The Divine Comedy* (Boston, 1965).

13. James Thomson, *Essays and Phantasies* (London, 1881), p. 92.

14. *Ibid.*, pp. 102-103.

15. My translation. (A.P.)

DANTE'S SATAN AND MILTON'S "BYRONIC HERO"

First published in Italica, *XLI, 2, 1964*

The difficulties one is apt to experience in reading Dante's *Commedia* in English are not limited to linguistic matters; they extend to the translation of the cultural and philosophical backgrounds of the work into an English frame of reference. In his well-known essay on Dante, T. S. Eliot has observed, for instance, that the English reader familiar with the Miltonic Satan is likely to come away from the 34th Canto of the Inferno with "the impression of a Devil suffering like the human damned souls" — an impression which is bound to disappoint any reader of the poem. The "Byronic hero" of *Paradise Lost*, says Eliot, makes us keenly aware of the contrast between the two representations and forces upon us the conclusion that "the *kind* of suffering experienced by the Spirit of Evil," as described by Dante, "should be represented as utterly different."[1]

To berate Eliot, as an Italian critic did, for such a conclusion is to create confusion.[2] Eliot may not have grasped Dante's full intention, but he was correct in being disappointed in a Satan who, in his perception, was suffering as a human being. Eliot himself points out that his impression may well be the result of a subconscious mental anachronism, an insistence upon preconceptions very different from what Dante intended to represent; one may even be led to agree that his disappointment merely betrays Eliot's incapacity to rid himself of modern ideas; but it is impossible for anyone with a fair knowledge of the text to accept the notion that Dante meant in fact to create the impression that disappointed Eliot.

Although unable to explain it adequately, Eliot seems to have instinctively understood that a Devil suffering like the human souls is not in keeping with

Dante's carefully structured topography of Hell. Only a superficial reader will fail to expect in Dante's Satan a *qualitative* change, a description consistent with the nature of the source of all evil. Dante expects his readers to see more than a poetic representation and to feel more than poetic justice at the sight of the ruler of the City of Dis. The King of Hell is not to be confused with his subjects, with those who have fallen under his rule.

In Canto XI of the Inferno, Dante adopts an Aristotelian scheme which distinguishes the three stages of sin as incontinence, vice or malice (*kakia*), and bestiality — a division which has its counterpart in continence, virtue, and divinity. This Aristotelian framework suggests that in the pit of Hell there will be something more than a mere intensification of suffering, just as at the height of Paradiso there will be more than mere intensification of joy. Bestiality, like divinity, is outside the pale of the human. It is to be expected, then, that in describing bestiality at its source Dante would attempt something different from what has gone before.

Canto XXXIV opens with a quotation from the great processional of the Church, the hymn sung at the approaching of the Cross — *Vexilla regis prodeunt* — only here the banners that advance belong not to the King of Heaven but the King of Hell — *Inferni*. The initial shock produced by this blasphemous inversion is intensified by the disorientation that follows. Darkness and heavy fog reduce visibility almost to zero; this, and the icy wind, force Dante to seek shelter at Virgil's side. Virgil warns him that he will now have to rally all his strength, but Dante is struck so forcibly by the confusion around him that all power is drained from him and he becomes speechless. He tells us all this quickly, describing in effect a double transcendence similar to that which he describes at the end of Paradiso, when he comes face to face with God. Not only is he powerless to describe what he sees, but he is powerless to describe his very feelings. His human faculties fail him completely. What he actually describes is a vision seen, not with human eyes but with another kind of sight, a vision which, like the vision of God, transcends human articulation. In the pit of Hell, Dante experiences an ecstasy before Evil:

> Io non morii, e non rimasi vivo
> pensa oramai per te, s'hai fior d'ingegno,
> qual io divenni, d'uno e d'altro privo. (25-27)

In prefacing his description of Satan with an account of the ecstatic nature of his experience, Dante is indeed preparing his readers for something extraordinary. There can be no doubt that he wishes to raise his readers' expectations.

All this may escape a first reading. Dante himself repeatedly warns his readers that they may well be disappointed — in fact, lost — if they read carelessly, superficially. This is especially true with regard to Cocytus, where Dante builds up the description on a series of contrasts and parallels which are meant, to suggest, throughout, other parts of the poem, particularly the last canto of the Paradiso. What may seem at first reading nothing more than "construction" or "cement" holding together isolated patches of poetry, asssumes an altogether different aspect when read with the end of the Paradiso fresh in mind, for the infinite suggestiveness of the last canto of the Inferno lies precisely in a careful juxtaposition of opposites. The technique is not wholly arbitrary; Dante's Satan has no real or positive attributes of his own — he can be described effectively only as a negation or denial of God.

Is Dante successful in his representation? Does he fulfill the expectations he has raised, or does he mislead us, as Eliot has suggested?

One thing is certain: the creature Dante sees embedded in the icy pit of Cocytus is *not* human. The three revolting heads, the six bat-like wings, the gigantic proportions of the figure as a whole suggest something inhuman, or, rather, sub-human. Dante stresses this by the use of words like *ceffo, bava, cresta, vipistrello, pelo, croste, verme*, all of which describe the lowest forms of animal life seen in their ugliest light. As the great critic Francesco De Sanctis has pointed out, Satan is the lowest rung on the ladder of spiritual blessings, somewhere between the human and the animal. He is pure instinct, pure appetite.[3] He is the antithesis of divinity — not animal, not human — outside the natural order of created beings. The bestiality of Satan is the result of his fall not from *human* goodness but from *divine* goodness. Dante does indeed want us to feel let down in the presence of Satan, not to the extent of aesthetic disappointment, however, but all the way, to the full realization of the measure of Lucifer's fall from grace. The creature who was once the brightest of the angels is now the most depraved of living things, the source of all sin, his ambition frustrated into almost ridiculous impotence, his beauty transformed into revolting ugliness. He who had been closest to God, almost pure act devoid of gross matter, has become the most abject of creatures, wholly material, almost paralyzed into inactivity.

Dante hammers on this contrast. The gigantic three-headed monster who once thought himself the equal of God has become the very antithesis of God — a grotesque caricature of the Holy Trinity. The very colors of the three monstrous heads recall their counterparts in the Triune God. And just as the human nature of Christ is visible in the blinding light of the Holy Trinity, so human nature at its worst is visible here, mangled and almost unrecognizable, in the foaming bloody jaws of Satan. Brutus, Cassius, and Judas are the sinners *par excellence,* inhuman in their betrayal, just as Christ is the perfect man, superhuman in his sacrifice on the cross.

There is, finally, the parallel between the political order of Heaven and that of Hell. Satan is *"regis . . . inferni,"* King of Hell but, at the same time, Emperor of the entire universe of sin, "lo imperador del doloroso regno." (28) The terminology is unmistakable: Satan rules within his prescribed limits in the same way that God rules. God too is both King and Emperor — King of Heaven and Emperor of the Universe. The political order, which is the most glorious attribute of the City of God, exists in some measure even in the City of Dis, for wherever there is a flicker of life there is some semblance of order. The repulsive creature whose bulk fills the dark icy pit of Cocytus is the political counterpart of God.

Seen as the dark antithesis of the light and love of God, Dante's Satan cannot fail to produce an impression at least as forceful as that produced by the "Byronic hero" of Milton's poem. The poetic language of the last canto of the Inferno is no less dramatic than the language of *Paradise Lost*. Dante, with the sensitive touch of a real poet, is here recalling the main theme of the work in a minor key, using discordant notes and jarring sounds to describe the full exhaustion of the lyrical melody.

But — admitting that Dante was concerned with depicting the suffering of Satan as qualitatively different from all the other suffering in the Inferno — can we insist that his Satan is as interesting and profound a representation as that of Milton? The obvious differences make it almost impossible, at first, to see what the two might have in common. Dante's Satan remains virtually immobile throughout. Milton's is moving continually, changing his form, scouting the heavens and the Garden of Eden, as well as Hell, assuming whatever shape best suits his purpose. Dante's Satan is grotesque; Milton's darkly sublime. Dante's Satan is repulsive; Milton's is admirable in his determination and his depth of feeling, in his sense of loyalty to those who depend on him and look to him for guidance and reassurance. Dante's Satan does not speak; Milton's is often eloquent. Dante's Satan has no redeeming feature; Milton's has the humanitarian impulses of a great leader. Dante's Satan arouses disgust; Milton's, at times, arouses something close to sympathy. It is not surprising to find that readers and critics of *Paradise Lost* (Dryden,[4] Burns,[5] and Blake,[6] to mention three of the more notable ones) have often identified Milton's Satan as the real hero of the poem. Surely there is something noble in the Unconquerable Will that in the face of utter darkness and despair will not yield to the Victor (Book I, 105-124), in the awful spirit who vows to continue eternal war "by fraud or guile," (Book I. 646) who despises all weakness as "miserable Doing or suffering" (Book I, 157-158), who refuses to be crushed by circumstances of place or time, who is able to recognize the force and the limits of his own ambition (Book I, 249-263) — the dauntless leader, bold in his planning and in the execution of his design, who "for the general safety" despises "his own." (Book II, 481-482) Milton's Satan has all the tragic grandeur of a Greek hero. His strength of purpose, misdirected as it is, arouses our admiration. And admiration gives way to a kind of pity as we watch the anguish of his spirit.

His defenses against the superior forces which have destroyed his glory and peace is tempered by an emotional sensitivity that calls forth our sympathy. The sight of his fellow spirits condemned to eternal pain because of his encouragement brings on remorse and passion which burst forth, in spite of self-scorn, in "tears, such as angels weep." (Book I, 620) His transgression is inexcusable, and yet this outburst against God is full of terrible pathos which stirs and disturbs the sensitive reader:

> . . . But he who reigns
> Monarch in Heav'n, till then as one secure
> Sat on his Throne, upheld by old repute,
> Consent or custome, and his Regal State
> Put forth at full, but still his strength conceal'd,
> Which tempted our attempt, and wrought our fall.
> (Book I. 637-642)

Perhaps the most impressive and moving quality of Milton's Satan is his appreciation of all that is good and beautiful. He is painfully sensitive to light and love; his despair is awakened sharply at the sight of Heaven and Eden. He cannot help remembering the goodness of God, "Heav'ns matchless King," who deserved "no such return" as he gave (Book IV, 41-42); he bemoans the fact that he was not ordained some inferior angel who might have escaped the '"unbounded hope" which has misled him (Book IV, 60). These thoughts inspire him to a kind of confession which, however, stops short of repentance: he yearns to ask forgiveness but dreads the shame he would suffer among those he seduced to his purpose and for whom he has assumed full responsibility. If he were to follow his natural instincts and submit to God, he would betray their trust. The spark of goodness which momentarily dullens his evil intention flares up in one last bright flame at the sight of Adam and Eve, in whom the "Divine resemblance" shines forth in all its radiance (Book IV, 364). Coming upon them, he is overwhelmed by their beauty and can only gaze in wonder. He experiences in their presence a kind of dark ecstatic love under whose influence he almost succumbs, ready to pity them. He is drawn to them almost in spite of himself; in a sense, *he* is lost to *them*, he becomes their silent wooer, vowing them his dark love and all that goes with it, for all eternity:

> Ah gentle pair, yee little think how nigh
> Your change approaches, when all these delights
> Will vanish and deliver ye to woe,
> More woe, the more your taste is now of joy;
> Happie, but for so happie ill secur'd
> Long to continue, and this high seat your Heav'n
> Ill fenc't for Heav'n to keep out such a foe
> As now is enterd; yet no purpos'd foe
> To you whom I could pittie thus forlorne
> Thought I unpittied. League with you I seek,
> And mutual amitie so streight, so close,
> That I with you must dwell, or you with me
> Henceforth; my dwelling haply may not please
> Like this fair Paradise, your sense, yet such
> Accept your Makers work; he gave it me,
> Which I as freely give; Hell shall unfold,
> To entertain you two, her widest gates,
> And send forth all her Kings. . . .
>   (Book IV, 366-384)

His sudden impulse to regain what he has lost, the force of his dark love are frustrated in the face of an immutable destiny. Milton's Satan, like Dante's, cannot undo the consequences of rebellion against God. He is, for all eternity, the absolute ruler of Hell:

> . . . Hells dread Emperour with pomp Supream,
> And God-like imitated State. . . .
>   (Book II, 510-511)

He cannot avoid assuming his "Imperial Sov'ranty" (Book II, 446), or escape the "Monarchal pride" (Book II,

428) which, accompanies it. Indeed, it is precisely his position of leadership, his intrinsically profounder understanding and greater capacity for feeling that enable him to estimate correctly the full impotence of his role and to recognize the full mockery of his existence:

> . . . The thought
> Both of lost happiness and lasting pain
> Torments him; round he throws
> His baleful eyes. . . .
> (Book II, 54-56)

The full realization of all he has lost finds its outlet in an impotent rage. Dante's Satan, in much the same way,

> Con sei occhi piangeva, e per tre menti
> gocciava il pianto e sanguinosa bava. (53-54)

In spite of the momentary glimmer of hope which flares up at the sight of the luminous heavens, Milton's Satan is doomed to renew his despair and hate:

> Be then his Love accurst, since love or hate
> To me alike, it deals eternal woe,
> Nay curs'd be thou; since against his thy will
> Chose freely what it now so justly rues.
> Me Miserable! Which way shall I flie
> Infinite wrath, and infinite despaire?
> Which way I flie is Hell; my self am Hell;
> And in the lowest deep a lower deep
> Still threatening to devour me opens wide,
> To which the Hell I suffer seems a Heav'n.
> (Book IV, 69-78)

He is tormented again at the sight of Adam and Eve:

> . . . O Hell! What doe mine eyes with grief behold
> In our room of bliss thus high advanc't
> Creatures of other mould. . . .
> (Book IV, 558-560)

His irresistible attraction to them brings him to the very edge of repentance. His hopes at this moment are at their peak; but the frustration that follows, the realization that he can never attain goodness is as dark and terrible as his hopes had been bright. From here on, he gives himself over completely to deceit and guile, directing all his energies to the accomplishment of his dark design, with the same impotent rage we witness in Dante's Satan as, embedded in the ice and filth of Cocytus, he mangles the bodies of the arch-traitors with his sharp fangs.

Milton's Satan, unlike Dante's, seems to reflect at moments all the inspiring pathos and attractive stoicism of a Brutus, a Macbeth, an Oedipus. His humanitarian instincts elevate him at times to something resembling a tragic hero — until we remember that, cut off from the love of God, such instincts (as St. Augustine reminds us) are pernicious and evil. And yet, read correctly, the two representations have much in common. Both know the full darkness of Hell because they have known the full light of Heaven. The extent of the suffering of Milton's Satan can be measured against the hopeless desire which is called forth at the sight of Heaven and Adam and Eve, just as the suffering of Dante's Satan can be measured effectively only against the light and love of the last canto of Paradiso. The darkness and cold despair which surround Dante's Satan is the same dark hopelessness which Milton's Satan gives expression to in his moments of desperate grief. The ice and darkness of Cocytus are simply projections of the hopelessness and despair in his heart. And in the heart of darkness and despair, the fate of Milton's Satan is as black and awful as that of Dante's Satan. For both, desire will never mature into hope of fruition; all action must dissolve into impotence, all despair must turn into rage. Stripped of the stoic grandeur and the stoic pride which seem at moments to raise him above his terrible doom, Milton's Satan betrays the same impotent rage which characterizes Dante's Satan — a rage which, though directed outward, invariably turns back in upon itself in a kind of Promethean fury. There is in both the same suppressed violence, the same gigantic hate held in check, the same icy despair. The truth stripped of its stoic trappings is simple: cut off from the light and love of God all life is perverted, all ambition thwarted, the highest goals of men and angels reduced to nothing and their noblest sentiments turned into bitter gall.

Dante's Satan is a *reductio ad absurdum* of the "Byronic hero" of Paradise Lost. Milton's Satan, if properly understood, does not detract from Dante's poetic representation but, rather, intensifies it. He gives expression to many and varied moods, to the most intense psychological inversions; he is capable of pity for others, love for beauty and goodness, and noble sentiments as well as self-pity, jealousy, pride and hatred for God. And yet, in the spectrum of his own experience, he is merely reflecting what Dante develops carefully and systematically through the many individual characterizations in the journey through Hell. The attraction of sin, the ever-diminishing vestiges of beauty, nobility, and stoic pride in those who sin, the growing impotence and rage of the malefactors as we move deeper and deeper into Dis are, in the Inferno, part of one single picture of the entire human experience of sin, conceived as a gradual diminution of Being. The bottom of Hell, the narrowest point in the truncated cone which is the graphic representation of the ultimate reaches of sin, is a point of almost no dimension, the point furthest removed from the light and love of God.

Dante's representation of Satan is the obvious logical conclusion of all that has gone before, but it is also the clear and unambiguous commentary of the whole. The reader who wishes to appreciate the full poetic impact of the last canto of the Inferno must bring with him not a *tabula rasa* but the wealth of poetic experience contained in the whole Inferno; and he must be able to project that dark experience against the light of the Paradiso. He must see the Inferno as the destructiveness of self-love, the negation of that caritas which radiates throughout the heavens; and he must see in Dante's Satan the extreme expression of that self-love, of the true nature of misdirected freedom which has cut itself off from the source of life. In the light of his vision of God, in whose depth

> . . . s'interna,
> legato on' amore in un volume,
> ciò che per l'universo si squaderna
> (*Par.* XXXIII, 85-87)

Dante's careful delineation of Satan reveals the same strokes of genius which make the last canto of the

Paradiso — in Eliot's words — "the highest point that poetry has ever reached or ever can reach."[7]

NOTES

1. T. S. Eliot, "Dante," *Selected Essays, 1917-1932* (New York, 1932), p. 212. The essay, like so much of Eliot's critical writing, is not only instructive but also good reading.

2. John V. Falconieri, "Il Saggio di T. S. Eliot su Dante," *Italica*, June 1957, pp. 75-78.

3. Francesco De Sanctis, *Antologia critica sugli scrittori d'Italia*, Luigi Russo, ed., Vol. I (Firenze, 1933), p. 155.

4. See Joseph Addison, *Criticism on Milton's Paradise Lost* (Westminster, 1895), p. 44.

5. See: James Thomson, "A Few Words About Burns," *Poems, Essays, and Fragments* (London, 1903), p. 89. Thomson quotes the following passage as characteristic of "the heroism of [Burns'] grave mood":

> Give me a spirit like my favorite hero, Milton's Satan. . . . I have bought a pocket Milton which I carry perpetually about with me in order to study the sentiments — the dauntless magnanimity, unyielding independence, and noble defiance of hardship in that great personage, Satan.

6. See Blake's famous utterance in "The Marriage pf Heaven and Hell," *Eighteenth Century Poetry and Prose*, Louis I. Bredvold, Alan D. McKillop, Lois Whitney, editors. (New York, 1939), p. 212:

> The reason Milton wrote in fetters when he wrote of Angels and God, and at liberty when of Devils and Hell, is because he was a true Poet and of the Devil's party without knowing it.

7. Eliot, p. 212.

DANTE AND MACHIAVELLI: POLITICAL "IDEALISM" AND POLITICAL "REALISM"

Based on a lecture delivered in New York, 1979

It is an ironic fact of history that the Italian Risorgimento — intrinsically an anti-papal movement — should have adopted as its standard-bearer and prophet the great poet who was officially recognized by Pope Benedict XV, early in the 20th century, as the poetic spokesman of the Catholic Church: *Aligherius noster est.* The claims of these two "opposing" factions — the secular and the religious — have never been seriously questioned; indeed, in themselves they are not necessarily in contradiction. A man can be patriotic without being accused of hypocrisy in his religious commitments. In this particular case, however, the secular faction — the Risorgimento — was essentially hostile to the Church (we have all seen pictures and statues of the *Bersaglieri* running toward Rome to reclaim it from the Pope).

There is an even greater irony in the fact that Dante should have become identified with the great secular movement of Italian unification, that the poet who thundered against a plurality of states should have become the champion — in the minds of many — of Italian nationalism. A 1961 editorial in the *Saturday Review*, commemorating the 100th anniversary of Italian unification, had this to say about Dante's role in the Risorgimento:

> A century ago, on March 17, 1861, the dream of Dante came true when the first Italian Parliament gathered in the ancient Piedmont city of Turin and proclaimed the Kingdom of Italy.

To identify Dante's dream of a Roman empire, patterned after the great empire of Augustus Caesar, with the Italy of Garibaldi and Mazzini is to turn the great poet's unambiguous political premise upside down. The error has, indeed, enjoyed embarrassing prominence for the last hundred years, especially on a popular level, but it is nothing more than a glamorous myth.

Dante's "dream" of a united Italy — a "dream" first attributed to him by the generation which opened the Renaissance — cannot, except by a long stretch of the imagination, be actually attributed to him. In their poetic exuberance, the leaders of the Risorgimento may certainly be excused for claiming Dante as their own, but the facts reveal a Dante very different from the one they created in their own image.

The error is understandable in a way. What could be simpler than identifying the great poet of the *Commedia* with the geographical entity whose vernacular he fashioned? But simple logic is not sufficient, in this case, to establish the equation which would make of Dante the prophet of modern Italy.

Dante is not the first Italian patriot but the last extreme internationalist of his day, a "one-world" advocate or, to use a modern parallel, a defender of an efficient, all-inclusive "United Nations" in which the *many* nations, however, are reduced to *one*, and in which moral authority is clear and unambiguous in the form of the Church's spiritual guidance. In his political views (as in his poetic theory) Dante represents the "summing up" of the middle ages. He is the last great spokesman of a cultural, political, and religious tradition which is consciously rejected in the generation that follows him. The hero-prophet of Italian nationalism is not Dante but Petrarch, whose friend Cola di Rienzo officially proclaimed the restored Roman "republic" in 1347.

Petrarch is the first to popularize the distinction between Italians (or, more properly, "Romans") and "barbarians" (all those outside the Italian peninsula). For Petrarch, the Italians represent the sacred remnant of ancient Rome. They are the chosen people, destined to revive the glory of the Roman republic of antiquity. The Germans, with their horrid manners, their indifference to classical art, their inability to fashion elegant Ciceronian prose, could not be accepted in the "elite" society of a sophisticated Latin Italy — according to Petrarch — unless, of course, they dropped their "Germanity" and made themselves over in the image of ancient Rome. This position, first articulated in popular form by Petrarch, has more or less prevailed in Italy. It was brought to the fore in the Risorgimento and, again, by Mussolini, who recalled ancient Roman symbols in the very name he adopted for his government. Fascism, whatever the judgment of history, was ideally a revival of the ancient Rome of Petrarch and the leaders of the Risorgimento. In this tradition, Dante has absolutely no place. He was well aware of the "nationalistic" arguments which were to gain popularity after him but rejected them emphatically and unequivocally.

When Dante berates the city-states of Genoa, Pisa, Venice, Milan, Florence, etc., he is addressing himself to political entities which were in fact self-sufficient: that is, each was independently capable of protecting itself against external and internal enemies and of providing for the economic prosperity of its people. The city-states Dante writes about had already, as in the case of Venice and Genoa, shown indications of what might be called "imperial" expansion. They are not the cities of today (no city in our modern world can be called "self-sufficient"); they were powerful communities capable of economic expansion and practicing high diplomacy on an international scale. By the 13th century, Genoa had attained coveted primacy in international trade; Venice too had its day; and Florence, under the extraordinary skill of the Medici, was to become the greatest "creditor nation" of its time, lending huge sums of money to monarchs and emperors, including the King of England.

Dante was well aware of the "national" conflicts around him. He recognized the self-sufficiency of the city-states, but his insistence that they give up their sovereignty was not, like Machiavelli's insistence later, based on the assumption that those communities could not defend themselves or carry on the activities of "sovereign" states. In his day, Machiavelli could make that assumption; but in Dante's time those city-states could still defend themselves and secure economic well-being. It was that very self-sufficiency which Dante condemned.

His arguments are set down clearly in his two greatest works, the *Commedia* and *De Monarchia* (On World Government), but his position is already established in earlier works. In the *Convivio* (Banquet), for example, he insists in no uncertain terms that peace can be realized only if "'the whole world . . . be a monarchy, that is one single princedom, having one prince." A world monarchy is essential, he tells us,

> to keep the kings contented within the boundaries of their kingdoms, so that there shall be peace between them, in which peace the cities may have rest, and in this rest the districts may love one another, and in this love the households may receive whatsoever they need, and when they have received whatsoever they need, man may live in happiness, which is that whereto man is born.

In the famous letter to Henry VII of Luxemburg, he reminds the German ruler of his role as head of a world empire: "the glorious dominion of the Romans," he asserts emphatically, "is confined neither by the frontiers of Italy nor by the coastline of three-cornered Europe.

The necessity for a world empire and the divine nature of such rule is worked out in all its details in *De Monarchia*. The argument can be summed up simply enough. God signified his approval of imperial government by the fact that Christ was born during the Roman Empire. The world "was never in a state of universal peace except under the monarch Divus Augustus, at which time there was a perfect monarchy." Under Augustus, and later under Justinian, the laws that were to govern the world were set down and codified. The laws are still available but the man who is to apply them is not at hand. And, as long as the emperor is not available to administer the laws inspired by God, the world will remain in darkness and chaos. The argument is driven home in the sixth canto of Purgatorio:

Cerca, misera, intorno dalle prode
le tue marine, e poi ti guarda in seno,

se alcuna parte in te di pace gode.
Che cal, perchè ti racconciasse il freno
   Giustiniano, se la sella è vota?
   Senz' esso fora la vergogna meno.

(Search, wretched one, around the shores
   of your seas, and then look inside you,
   if any part of you enjoys peace.
What does it matter that Justinian fixed the reins for you,
   if the saddle is empty?
   Were it not so, the shame would be less.)

The Empire, like the Church, is for Dante divinely ordained. Rome, that gave peace to the world, had at one time two suns: the imperial ruler and the Vicar of Christ. Their authority comes from God, and their power is properly used insofar as the Emperor directs men to their temporal ends and the Pope, to their spiritual ends. When the two powers became confused — Dante reminds his readers both in *De Monarchia* and the *Commedia* — men lose sight of their proper ends, and wars and chaos make the attainment of happiness impossible. Dante reinforces the argument, logically, by pointing out (naively perhaps) that the Emperor, having complete power over mankind, can want nothing more and therefore can give his full attention to putting the world in order. He is not intrinsically good; but by virtue of his power and already possessing all that he can possibly want, he is beyond the temptations of greed.

> Where there is naught to be desired, cupidity is impossible; for when their objects are destroyed, the passions cease to exist. But since the monarch's jurisdiction is bounded only by the ocean, there is naught that he can desire. This is not the case with other princes whose principalities are bounded by others. . . . Whence it follows that the monarch is of all mortals the most capable of justice.

Only one man fits the bill: the German emperor "chosen" by God and named by the German electors. Only one sovereign can assume effective charge of the world empire patterned after the great empire of Augustus, in which the beautiful peninsula of Italy would always enjoy privileged status as the "garden of the Empire." With one temporal ruler to show mankind the way to happiness on earth and one spiritual leader to guide mankind to eternal happiness, the world will once more enjoy peace; and only then will we be able to carry on the cultural and intellectual pursuits which dissension and wars necessarily interrupt.

What Dante conceived may best be described as an all-inclusive federation of states, with ultimate power resting in one, all-embracing, sovereign Empire.

In the *Commedia*, Dante takes up the same arguments of *De Monarchia*, hurling bitter invectives against all who tried to place obstacles in the path of the Emperor. The poem is, in a sense, the grand iliad which describes the struggle that destroyed the two great powers of Church and Empire and made possible the rise of the modern states. Again and again in his famous epic, Dante reminds his readers of the chaos which has come about with the Church's arrogation of temporal power. Again and again he reminds us that the sword of the Emperor and the crozier of the Vicar of Christ must never be joined. We know with what respect and nostalgia he refers to the Hohenstaufens (Barbarossa, Frederick II, Manfred, and Conradin), with what unswerving judgment he damns both Philip IV of France and Pope Boniface VIII, whose ambitions and fears drove them to ally themselves against the Emperor and brought about his defeat. The masque he witnesses and describes in all its suggestive details at the top of the mountain of Purgatorio is a symbolic representation of the Universal Church so weakened and corrupted by the struggle with the Hohenstaufens that it falls prey, in its state of exhaustion, to the demands of the French ruler — the first "national" sovereign of the modern world. The Pope, unable to protect himself from the "terzium gaudens," the third party who rose up to enjoy the spoils, was forced to move from Rome to Avignon, where he was made to serve the interests of the French King in the capacity of a private chaplain.

What Dante describes is, in effect, the end of the medieval Church. In our modern world, the church (fragmented, like the Empire, into a plurality of independent units), is subject to national states that determine whether or not it will be tolerated (as in the United States), persecuted (as in China), or accepted as a national institution (as in England and Spain).

Dante's description of the masque is accurate in all its details, but he does not, will not, accept it as ultimate fact. In spite of the reality of the "Avignon captivity," he looks forward to the coming of Henry VII of Luxemburg, citing reverently side by side, at crucial moments in his poem, Virgil and Roman history, the testament of the glorious empire divinely ordained by Providence and Scriptures, the testament of the eternal empire of Heaven. There can be no doubt as to what he felt about those popes and rulers, "Italian" and foreign, who sought to maintain their own power at the expense of the Emperor's. He was witnessing the birth of the modern world but never resigned himself for a moment to the obvious. Indeed, he did everything in his power to stem the tide.

One cannot say what Dante would have said or done had he lived to see the Risorgimento. We do know that he reserved his severest punishment in the Inferno for the betrayers of the imperial ideal in antiquity, identifying them, in his poetic and moral scale of values, with the betrayer of Christ. In the icy pit of Hell, Satan himself administers eternal justice to Cassius and Brutus, the betrayers of the Empire, mangling them in his bestial jaws together with Judas, the betrayer of Christ — eloquent testimony to Dante's grand but hopeless dream.

The great spokesman for Italian nationalism is not Dante, but Machiavelli. The uncompromising realist, the founder of modern political theory, the champion of *realpolitik* was no less determined than Dante in taking up his cause: only, in his case the cause was not imperial rule but a strong unified Italy as part of the plurality of nations.

For a while, in the 16th century, Machiavelli's name was synonymous with the devil, because his political philosophy seemed so ruthless and cynical. It had to be: the Italy of his day was still suffering the ills described three centuries earlier by Dante. Machiavelli's solution to the problem, however, was very different.

For Machiavelli, the only realistic solution to a fragmented country was a unified sovereign nation that could take its place as an equal in the ongoing power struggle between sovereign states. He did not minimize the difficulties in the way of achieving that goal; he accepted the hard realities and made the most of them, turning them to his purpose. For this he has been severely criticized: his name is apt to inspire heated controversy at any meeting where there are idealists who argue for "things are they ought to be" and hard realists who accept "things as they are."

Historically, the successful "Machiavellian" is never identified as such. To identify a man as such means that he failed as a ruler or minister in what he set out to do. Cesare Borgia certainly was a "Machiavellian," but had he succeeded, for starters, in unifying, the region of Lombardia (as he almost did), he might have been honored as a hero. Thomas Cromwell, the 16th-century minister of Henry VIII, who succeeded Thomas More in that office, was a "Machiavellian" — perhaps the most ruthless of all political figures of the modern world: his strategies to free England from foreign control and insure its future as a major player with other nations succeeded, but Henry VIII did not give him a chance to emerge as a national hero. Winston Churchill, who said at a time of crisis that he would "make a friend of the devil himself to save England," emerged, in our time, as the savior of the British Isles in World War II.

The political condition of man, for Machiavelli, is rooted in his human nature. And, although he was not a religious man, he saw human nature as St. Augustine and Dante saw it: intrinsically greedy, selfish, mean, and hypocritical. Man instinctively seeks his own interests and will do anything to get what he wants, unless someone stops him.

As a psychologist, he was painfully accurate. Men, he pointed out, are much more willing to accommodate themselves to defeat than to die heroically.

We honor heroes and saints precisely because they are so rare. Politically, this notion is elaborated in many ways in *The Prince*, that little book which has been so provocative and influential ever since it appeared and which is still, today, excellent and profitable reading. In it we are reminded, for example, how men react when a town or country is captured. If the conqueror wants to be sure of "winning the peace," the most efficient way to set about doing it is to destroy, kill if necessary, the leading citizens who, deprived of their former wealth and status, can become nuclei of sedition. That's terrible, we say. Machiavelli anticipates our reaction and explains the alternatives.

If you leave such people to their own devices, he tells us, you run the risk of being overthrown and perhaps killed yourself. By getting rid of your enemies you set an example which out of fear the rest of the people you have overcome will easily understand and accept. After that, you can begin to make concessions aimed at getting, finally, the "consent of the governed" — because no ruler can lead a people for very long if he doesn't ultimately have their cooperation. The initial harsh measures will soon be forgotten, especially if things get better after that. The worst thing is to start out kindly and then betray the people you have won by having to resort to hard tactics. If that happens, your actions will be interpreted as a sign of weakness. The other way is better, human nature being what it is.

But to succeed requires tremendous understanding and cunning. In the initial process of transition from conqueror to acknowledged ruler, the conqueror naturally is apt to arouse strong feelings of hatred in some, if not all, those he has conquered. This is the moment of danger because (Machiavelli the psychologist explains) people will do almost anything when moved by hatred. They often risk their lives to avenge those they have lost fighting the enemy/conqueror, so hatred is to be avoided at all costs. Still, the conqueror cannot expect to be accepted and loved for a very long time, if ever; and even if that happens it will not insure his rule because love, like hate, is a very personal emotion which begins and ends in the heart of the individual and cannot be controlled one way of another outside him. So the good ruler, the successful ruler, must inspire, says Machiavelli, not love or hate but *fear*. Only fear keeps people in check; fear does not begin and end in the heart of the individual, but is motivated in such a way that the ruler can control it absolutely. Fear insures obedience; and obedience, though not the best kind of relationship, is essential, especially in that period of adjustment to the new ruler.

What of the ruler's relations with the rest of the world? Here Machiavelli describes the famous beast-man in the maxim about the lion and the fox. The ruler must have strength, he says, but he must not rely on that alone, because there are times when even physical strength can be undermined. He must also be cunning, like the fox, in order to recognize his advantage and take it without show of force, if possible. With cunning he can control situations and turn defeat into victory. Cunning means withdrawing from a difficult spot, when the advantage is lost, and using other tactics. It means, if you're English, letting the Iranians have their oil but setting up an initial blockade to make it impossible for then to export it . . . until they have made a deal with you. It means, if you're French, getting out of North Africa rather than fight a propaganda war as the French "oppressor" against the Algerians. It means keeping your strength in reserve for other, more meaningful confrontations. It means inspiring internal difficulties among your enemies and provoking them indirectly by promoting — secretly perhaps — dissentions in their midst. Cunning is a sharp weapon and the successful ruler knows how and when to use it. But the need for a show of strength must never be ignored. The two go hand in hand.

The example Machiavelli uses in *The Prince*, as the epitome of strength and cunning is Cesare Borgia. He praises Borgia's handling of an insurrection among his captains. The efficient commander-in-chief had managed with fox-like cunning to woo the defectors back, making a show of forgiving them and restoring them to their former status. Then, after a conciliatory conference and a feast to celebrate the reunion, before the night was over, he had them all killed.

Machiavelli reports the story with undisguised approval: so long as the malcontents were allowed to live, they remained potential troublemakers. And even if they themselves weren't thinking of rising against their leader again at some future date, others might be tempted to try the same thing, if amnesty had indeed been granted the defectors. Borgia made sure that would not happen. All possibility of future rebellion was aborted.

The most quoted of Machiavelli's precepts — "the end justifies the means" — has often been misinterpreted to mean that whatever is required to reach a "good" end is justified. This conclusion leads to serious error and forces conclusions diametrically opposed to Machiavelli's intention.

Machiavelli himself warns us against such misinterpretation, showing us — in his dramatic masterpiece, *Mandragola* — where it can lead. In what is perhaps the most extreme articulation of human nature at its worst, the most ironic "comedy" ever written, the embittered former ambassador and statesman — the man who had enjoyed the trust and honors of the Florentine government; who had devoted years of loyal service to his people, only to be unceremoniously tossed aside when others took over — dramatizes the depths to which a human being can fall when he justifies what he craves.

Mandragola shows everyone getting by deft maneuvering what he or she wants. Nicia, the old, impotent husband needs a son who will inherit his wealth. His beautiful young wife is talked into being seduced by an admirer in order to give her husband the son he wants. The wife's mother encourages her daughter to commit adultery and thereby secure their places in the household as guardians of the heir. The wife's confessor, tricked into supporting the plot, cites Scriptures to get the seemingly pious wife to cooperate. The young admirer works out the fantastic plan that lets the old man think he can get his wife to conceive if she drinks a magic potion made from the mandrake root. The trouble, the creator of this fantastic tale explains, is that the first man to sleep with the woman after she drinks the magic potion, will draw the poison into himself and die. The husband, of course, must be spared: they will find a homeless beggar, who no one will ever miss, and force him to sleep with the woman and draw the poison from her, before Nicia takes over and makes her conceive. Of course, the beggar will be the young lover in disguise. The plot is a typical Plautian intrigue, but it has the added dimension of an ingenious exercise in high diplomacy. Everyone gets what he or she wants, without a hitch.

The play is Machiavelli's most bitter statement about human nature. It is also the most dramatic example of what happens when society breaks down and everyone seeks his own "good." Written, as we said, when Machiavelli;'s fortunes were at their lowest, as he waited in vain to be recalled into the political arena, the play reflects all the frustrations and bitterness of the restless outsider; but it is perfectly consistent with Machiaveli's political philosophy.

Mandragola depicts in all its horrors what can happen when "the end justifies the means" is used to justify personal behavior. The lesson is clear: when there are no restraints to check human appetites, society is threatened in every way. The play drives home the point that only *one end* can justify the ugly things that often have to be done to maintain a healthy society: *the safety of the state and the well-being of its people.* Whatever cruel measures Cesare Borgia employed were justified, in Machiavelli;'s eyes, in the light of Borgia's ambition to unify the various regions and bring peace to the Italian peninsula. If some terrible things had to be done to achieve that end, those means were justified in terms of that ultimate goal.

A similar goal, we can say, motivated Thomas Cromwell to persecute the most pious of the monastic orders, destroying the best among them to insure that the rest would easily follow suit. By doing so, he freed England from the influence of Rome, strengthened the national purpose, and brought about British control of the seas. The result was England's destruction of Catholic Spain's Armada and the beginning of a world-wide empire for Britain.

A modern parallel may be found in our own strategies to bring about an end to World War II. In the interest of American safety and to insure victory, we created and dropped the first atomic bomb on Japan.

Machiavelli is not advocating ugly solutions in and for themselves. He begins almost every chapter of *The Prince* with reminders that the ideal solution is always to be preferred — but when that fails, other strategies must be considered. He doesn't sit in judgment; he simply tells us that the hard realities have to be faced and carried out. Even Aristotle tells us (in the *Rhetoric*, where he explains the "art of persuasion" or, in our modern context, "propaganda") that you'd better know your enemy and try to beat him at his own game.

Mandragola presents the "comic" paradox of the tragic world of *The Prince*: it ends "happily" as a *commedia* should — everyone gets what he or she wants, each having adjusted, in this case, to execrable means to insure personal well-being. The monk agrees to allow an abortion as a prelude to much worse. Nicia is ready to accept the "murder" of a stranger to get his heir. His wife Lucretia is ready to commit adultery to insure her place in the household. Her mother presses her to take on a lover who will give her a child that Nicia will think is his. The Plautian intrigue turns into an obscene reality that is almost unbearable.

Machiavelli's realistic scenario reflects a fragmented society where "anything goes." Where effective leadership is missing, human nature succumbs to its lowest instincts. Without the restraints of a properly organized, self-sufficient sovereign state, people will not hesitate to follow their most egotistical impulses, to satisfy their most selfish, lowest desires.

For Machiavelli, political independence, the

acquisition of a "separate and equal" status among the powers of the earth, was the only possible solution to the social and political demoralization of the Italians. Borgia's ambition — whatever its motivation — would have served to destroy the petty egoism of scattered rulers who preferred their own personal advantage to national unity. Without a Borgia, Italy was what England would have been without a William the Conqueror, without an Edward I, without a Thomas Cromwell. Borgia could have brought about the *forced* unity of a conqueror, and would gradually have turned it into a *felt* unity, the prelude to government by discussion — but it was not fated to happen that way. The strong Prince was gone, the virtues of the protectors, producers, and governors (to use Plato's classifications) — temperance, honor, and prudence — could not be counted on to bring peace to warring factions.

In *Mandragola* we have the ironic peace of acquiescence and self-indulgence. The lesson of *The Prince* — of political expediency and boldness for a large purpose — is turned upside down in a drama of private vices rewarded through ingenuity turned to obscene ends.

The opening song of the play is the perfect articulation of the political paradox we are about to witness. In a setting similar to that of Boccaccio's *Ninfale fiesolano*, we get this epicurean philosophy of life:

Because we know that life is short
And we know what a weight of care
Living and striving, each of us must bear,

We idle away the length of our years
Pursuing each whim without measure;
For he who denies himself pleasure,
To live a life of anguish and tears,
Must be naively blind,
Ignoring how the world deceives,
And what devices fortune weaves
To overtake and to ensnare mankind.

We've chosen to flee from such sordid cares;
And, far from this sad world's confusion
We now live in festive seclusion,

Happy youths and nymphs. With our tuneful airs
And merry rhymes, we gather in your sight
So far from our accustomed way,
Only to keep this holiday
— And to enjoy your company tonight.

In the light of our argument, the concluding stanza of
this song becomes an ironic commentary:

But the name of your ruler also draws
Us here — in whom the bright reflection
Of virtues of divine perfection
Is visible. Those virtues are the cause
Of your well-being here below.
They guarantee your worldly gains,
And they secure the peace that reigns;
So thank him from whom your blessings flow.
(My translation)*

The ruler secures the good life through peace. But the
good life, the blessings of peace, are in the given context
nothing more than private indulgence. In the stock
phrases of the time, Machiavelli manages to flatter the
patron before whom the play — wherever it is shown —
unfolds; but, within the stereotype, there is also the
subtle reminder that Italy, in fact, is *not* in a condition of
peace, and that the "sad world's confusion" — like the
plague described at the beginning of the *Decameron* — is
waiting to overwhelm us. The "peace that reigns" is an
illusion that will disappear as soon as the pleasant
interlude is over. The ruler described is any one of
several real individuals, of course; his name may change,
depending on where the play is being shown and in
whose court Machiavelli is staying, but the circumstances
remain pretty much the same. Still, for the moment, he is
potentially the ideal prince who has it in his power to
restore his pleasure-seeking subjects to their purposeful
tasks, in a society structured to last and flourish as an
organic whole,

In spite of their very different arguments,
Machiavelli and Dante are basically in agreement as to
the need for strong and unified rule. For Dante that rule
is divinely ordained to be held by the German emperors

who will make of the diversity of nations, a single world empire. For Machiavelli that rule resides in the national states, where a balance of power insures restrains and therefore peace. Dante sees the plurality of nations, in particular the city-states of Italy, as an obstacle to world peace; Machiavelli too sees the fragmented Italy of his day as the great obstacle to peace, but his answer is not a restored medieval world empire but a strong unified country that can stand on its own as part of the family of modern nations. Dante is the idealist, the visionary who yearns, impossibly, for the restoration of imperial rule; Machiavelli is the hard-core realist who "tells it like it is," reminding every age that national self-interest must prevail. Dante, like St. Augustine, sees the world as a vale of tears: political idealism must eventually give way to divine providence. Machiavelli's premise is the same, but without any divine intervention to insure a happy ending.

From another, related point of view, *realpolitik* marks the beginning of that pioneering effort which was soon acclaimed by Sir Francis Bacon as the scientific spirit that ought to animate the scientist in his study of natural phenomena. It is Machiavelli's realism that we see reflected in Galileo's *Two New Sciences* and Gian Battista Vico's *The New Science*. That commitment, to see "things as they are," not "as they ought to be" is still the guiding principle of the modern world.

Dante and Machiavelli produced their great works in the midst of personal frustration, hoping against hope to regain some measure of acceptance in their beloved Florence. Machiavelli's fate may have been less harsh than Dante's (he was never forced to wander alone in a hostile world); but in the end, the circumstances of their private lives grow dim in the light of their extraordinary achievements.

For the *Commedia* teaches us more than a political and moral lesson; it makes us interpret our own motives and actions in s new light. *Mandragola* and *The Prince* are more than invectives against political realities and graceless human nature bent on satisfying its every whim; they force us to examine the deepest recesses of our soul. In the "idealism" of the *Commedia*, we recognize our full potential; in the "realism" of *The Prince* and *Mandragola*, we acknowledge our weaknesses and failures, and avoid hypocrisy. Their impact goes beyond praise of literary mastery.

---

* *Machiavelli's Mandragola*, trans. Anne and Henry Paolucci, with an Introduction by Henry Paolucci. First published by The Liberal Arts Press, 1957, currently in 40th printing (Paramount).

THE COSMOPOLITAN AGE OF DANTE AND HIS DREAM OF RESTORED IMPERIAL RULE

Based on lectures delivered at New York University, 1951.

Dante lived in an age that was genuinely cosmopolitan. Throughout the Mediterranean up to Norway and Iceland and even as far as Greenland, there was one religion, universal agreement on science and scientific laws, one dominating philosophy, one language. A student could go from the University of Bologna to that of Paris or Oxford, without having to learn a new language, or having to adopt a new conception of moral conduct, or of science, of art or philosophy. Setting aside linguistic differences that modern students have to deal with when they go to study abroad, think of the other cultural differences they or anyone who moves from one country to another has to cope with. A lawyer educated in Italy or in Poland can't possibly use his training effectively in the United States; he has to pass the Bar exam here in order to qualify — which means studying all over again. A German student of philosophy coming to Columbia or New York University would feel as though he'd landed on another planet: there is absolutely no meeting ground for American philosophers rooted in pragmatism and German philosophers whose training is essentially in "idealism." It was this cosmopolitanism that made 19th century reformers and writers like Carlyle, Ruskin, Morris, dream longingly of the unity of the middle ages.

But there was another side of the 13th century picture that was less attractive. Underneath all the cosmopolitanism was a political point of difficulty. It was not a struggle between exclusive factions in absolute opposition, like two different ways of life. It was not Democracy against Fascism or against Communism. It was a sort of family quarrel, as if a mother and father were to contest one another's right to control the behavior of their children. The quarrelers in this conflict agreed on the purpose of life, on the form of government, on moral values, on the allotment of duties to the members of the Christian family: they disagreed only as to who should have the last word. There are not many occasions when a last word is necessary, but it is vital to know who should have it, when it *is* necessary. Think of the Supreme Court's decisions compared with the many decisions of the lower courts and of individuals, families, councilmen, state representatives, congressmen, senators, captains, generals, etc.: they are few but extremely important because the Supreme Court has the last word and all other decisions must somehow accord with that.

The quarrel was between the universal Empire and the universal Church. They were in agreement on everything except who would have the last word. To those living today, such a struggle may not be of vital interest; we don't have before us a Church and State contending for power. The temporal powers in the modern world have the last world. In the nations where there is separation of Church and State, as in the United States, it is the State that determines that separation. In those nations where there is an official religion, like England, it is the State that gives official status to the religion. In those nations where the Church is suppressed, it is once again the State that decides. Nowhere in the Western world does the Church have the last word, and most of us are not sorry that this is the case. The Church itself that fought so hard to have the last word in Dante's time renounced that ambition within a political context, around 1870.

Both sides agreed that each had duties of its own and that these were separate and distinct. One provided temporal guidance, the other spiritual guidance. Still, they kept interfering with one another. The Emperor insisted that the Church's spiritual leadership was necessary — but don't try to control *me*! The Pope would answer: If you don't behave like a good Christian and follow my precepts, you don't deserve to rule our Christian subjects and as their spiritual leader I will instruct them to disobey you.

A current example may help to grasp the relationship I have described.

The United Nations, which, like the medieval Church, claims moral authority over its members, is made up of separate member nations, each with temporal authority and power. These member nations have equal "moral" authority in the U. N. — each of them has one "moral" vote — but they are very unequal in their temporal strength and power. Cuba and the United States both have one vote in the U. N., but the United States and Cuba are not equal in temporal strength, just as Hungary is not the equal of Russia. So it was in the medieval Church. All temporal rulers, great and small, were equally members of the Church, but they were not all equal in temporal power. The giant among them was the Empire. It was the strongest of the member subjects of the Church; in the 13th century it could enforce its will against the rest of the world. But the Emperor was not prepared to do that; he wanted to remain a member in good standing of Mother Church, just as the United States prefers to comply with the U. N. and not carry out crucial decisions without its approval.

In dealing with this great temporal ruler, the medieval Church found itself in a position similar to that of the U. N. today, in dealing with the United States. Some members of the Church were altogether hostile to the Emperor, but these were in a minority, like the Russian bloc in the U. N. was for a time a minority in opposition to the United States. Most ecclesiastical authorities gave their moral approval to the Emperor. They were worried about what he might do, like the British and French and Indian and Near Eastern members of the U. N. are worried about what the United States means to do, but they went along.

The parallel ends there. At a certain moment, the Church decided that the giant in its midst was asking too much and withheld its moral consent. In response, the Emperor took matters into his own hands and thereafter tried to suppress the moral authority of the Church, now used against him, by "stacking the court." The Church fought the attempt of the Emperor to control it by setting up a bloc of lesser nations against the Emperor. This bloc was head by the French king. Sanctioned by the Church, it succeeded in defeating the German Emperor. But the victory was short-lived for the Church. Drained by the hard struggle that had just ended, it was in no position to ward off new attacks by the lesser nations, vying to take the Emperor's place in the vacuum that had been created. Lesser rulers who had been content to cooperate with the Church and had accepted its moral authority in the past suddenly presented a new challenge. The Emperor's defeat made the protection of the Church no longer necessary. Predictably, they began to assert their independence. This moment marks the end of the Universal Church and Universal Empire and the beginning of our modern independent sovereign states The first nation to emerge from the momentous struggle for supremacy between Church and Empire was France.

The moment also marks the end of a cultural unity: the common language, art, philosophy, science, the universal values, the entire cultural heritage of the middle ages were soon to suffer drastic changes. It was a major turn in the history of the Western world.

The cosmopolitanism of the middle ages was deeply-rooted and had emerged slowly, organically. It was not, like the U. N. charter, the result of a San Francisco conference, where rules were drawn up with the hope that the nations of the world would respect them. It was the gradual, thoughtful acquisition of over 2,000 years, the culmination of a long process that began with Homer, Thales, the sophists and Socrates, developed through Plato and Aristotle. the stoics and neo-Platonists, then passed through the Roman Empire into a synthesis with Hebraic-Christian revelation, on to the Germanic barbaric culture which formed the basis of modern nations. In the Christian civilizations of the middle ages, all Greco-Roman culture capable of surviving found its place: in St. Augustine, the stoic-platonic tradition was firmly established on a Christian basis; with Justinian, Roman law found its place in the Christian culture; with the Scholastics, Aristotelian thought was assimilated.

A major change had to do with the concept of *rule* or *government.*

When the Germans invaded the Roman world, they entered upon a culture dominated socially and politically by the concept of "natural law," as formulated by the Roman jurists. Recently the term has been used to refer to the laws that govern falling bodies, the motion of the stars and planets, and other physical phenomena; but originally, the term was applied to the laws of human nature and how human conduct should conform to those laws. Aristotle was the first to use the term in this sense. Natural law for physical objects had to accord with the nature of those objects; natural law for human beings had to accord with human nature.

The natural law for a stone is that it should fall if there is nothing obstructing it. The natural law for water is to seek its own level. For fire, that it should rise. And so on. For a law to be natural it has to operate in all places and at all times, other things being equal (as modern science likes to remind us). According to Aristotle, human nature is *rational* and therefore natural law for human beings has to be a rational law, according to human nature.

This concept underwent a number of changes before the Germanic invasions. The first change was at the hands of the stoics. They extended the meaning of natural law to include those activities that man shares with the animals. The stoics were the first great cosmo-politans — the first to oppose the ancient distinction between barbarian and civilized people, between masters and slaves. They insisted upon the absolute natural equality of all men. In their enthusiasm for equality they tended, like our dog-lovers of today, to extend their sympathies beyond the human race, to include all animals. They acted upon this moral principle, with unfortunate cultural effects. Natural law tends to lose its rationalistic aspect when it is made to cover the condition of animals as well as men.

A more serious change was the result of Hebraic-Christian influences, especially the idea of man's fall from grace. Under the influence of the stoics, the Christian philosophers and jurists began to distinguish between the law of nature and the law of fallen nature. By natural law, for instance, all men should be absolutely equal: there should be no rulers, no laws governing another human being's behavior, no distinction of employers and workers, of masters and slaves, no concept of crime and punishment, no laws of commerce and trade.

For Aristotle, the relationship of ruler and subject, master and slave, buyer and seller, employer and worker was a natural one. The stoics, on the other hand, did not include these relationships under natural law, animals couldn't be included in all of them. Laws covering such relationship were, they said, matters of convention when they were good laws, matters of force when they were bad ones. The Christians added the idea that such laws were the result of fallen nature. Thus transformed by the stoics and Christians, the concept of natural law became the basis of the late Roman Empire at the time it fell to the Germans.

This concept of law, with its multiple applications, was compiled into a great *Corpus* or Body of Laws during the reign of the Emperor Justinian (629). For his own benefit, he added this important amendment: Because of man's fallen nature, it was impossible for man to regulate his affairs without God's direct help. Because of the fall from grace, man could not only pass bad laws, he could even make good laws operate badly. To remedy the situation, he said, God has designated a *living law* and that living law resides in the Imperial power. It makes no difference how an emperor comes to power, whether by general election or by conquest or by inheritance: his power, so long as he is allowed to exercise is, comes directly from God. And since God rules through the Christian Emperor, the Christian Emperor's *will* must be regarded as absolute law.

Justinian included such statements in his Body of Laws, but he didn't insist on them because there was no need to do so. He had other traditional, legal grounds for being the Absolute Ruler; but he also wanted *sanctified* rule. He wanted to have supreme spiritual authority as well, moral and spiritual justification for his temporal actions. Because he had done so much for the growing Church — following his predecessors' example, especially Constantine — the Pope allowed his claim. It opposed it only tacitly, by cautious moral reproofs, when the Emperor behaved in such a way as to violate the revealed moral laws which served as a basis for the Christian Church. All this was tolerable, especially since Justinian had his headquarters in the East, in Constantinople, and the Church was in Rome: distance helped avoid serious confrontations. Moreover, the Church was content to allow the claim in exchange for the prestige and authority it gained by good relations with the Imperial court.

When the Germans arrived into the Mediterranean world, the Church was forced to review its relationship to Imperial rule and laws. Roman law had been assimilated and Christianized by the Church, but now the Church had to assimilate and Christianize another kind of law. The Germans did not allow their rulers absolutism, such as the Roman emperors enjoyed. They ruled by *dynasty*. The ruler had to belong to one of the few families that had traditionally held power. His personal qualifications did not matter, providing his family claims were good. This dynastic concept had no parallel in the Greco-Roman world. There a son could succeed his father as ruler, not because he was the son of the previous ruler or because he belonged to a certain family, but because he had been selected to do so. Rulers might carry the same family name but rarely were of the same family: they were "adopted" sons or protegés. The emperor would select a promising young man, bring him up at court to study affairs of state and war, and so prepare him to take over imperial responsibilities.

Not only was the concept of dynastic rule alien to the people the Germans conquered; the dynastic rulers themselves could make no claims such as Justinian had made: their *will* was not *law*. They were themselves subjects and came under the same laws as the rest of the people. Their concept of law was different as well. It was what their forefathers had always done: *custom*. The ruler, like his subjects, had to follow tradition; he was merely an executive, enforcing custom.

Coming into the medieval world, the Germans discovered that their traditional tribal customs were inadequate for governing the conquered people spread out over a large area, with a culture acknowledged to be superior by the invaders themselves. They realized that they had to learn quickly the Roman concept of natural law as formulated by Justinian and sought out Roman jurists for the purpose.

A more important change was brought about by their contact with ecclesiastical authorities. If the German rulers wanted to be Christian rulers — and they did want that — they would have to acknowledge in some way Christian laws as revealed in the old and New Testaments. But how could their people, who respected and adhered to their tribal laws, be made to respect and adhere to another kind of law? A modern example might be: How can the Russian people who have lived by the laws of totalitarianism be made to follow and respect the regulations set down by the United Nations? The Church attempted to solve the problem by bringing the German ruler under its direct control through *anointment*. This meant that the ruler, in effect, was elevated into the clergy. Anointment meant additional prestige for the ruler who, already respected by his people, now became a missionary of God's will. In this role he came, of course, under the direct control of the head of the clergy, the Bishop of Rome. The arrangement served everyone's purpose for a long time. It helped the Church to Christianize the invading hordes that swept over the Roman world. Whenever there were contests between rulers, the Church could decide the issue by anointing one of the contenders. Where there were many small groups organized separately in tribes the Church could press for unity among them by anointing one and favoring him over the rest. In this way, the Church remade, with the help of outsiders, a new Roman Empire on the ruins of the old. The process culminated in the coronation by the Pope of Charlemagne as Emperor of the entire Christian-Roman world.

After Charlemagne, disintegration began. His successors fought over their inheritance, at the same time that new invaders attacked the continent: Norsemen from the North, Magyars from the East, Moslems from the South. Wars disrupted communications, the central political authority could no longer reach out effectively to outlying regions, the Church could no longer control its bishops and subordinate clergy. People were driven more and more to rely on the strong men among them for leadership and protection. The age of *feudalism* had begun.

A similar fragmentation was taking place within the Church, although there is no name given to it. The results were different in different parts of Europe. In France, political fragmentation reached its maximum, while ecclesiastical fragmentation was comparatively slight. The prelates of France continued to exert a great deal of authority over the many petty rulers that arose. In Germany, on the other hand, ecclesiastical fragmentation was greater than political fragmentation and the prelates were almost universally subjected to the petty rulers. In Italy, the fragmentation became a kind of feudalism in the south and resulted in the extraordinary development of city-states or communes in the north and central part of the country.

In Rome, the Papacy became subject to the factions contending for the rule of the city: the Bishop of Rome could no longer function effectively. As a result, the French ecclesiastical authorities, though strong, fell into abuses. In Germany, where the prelates were weak, they were subjected altogether to the will of the temporal ruler. The situation spread: in some parts of the world the clergy was corrupt because of temporal control; elsewhere, temporal rule was corrupt because it was unrestrained by the clergy; and Rome, the center of ecclesiastical and moral authority, could not function at all.

Not until the 11th century did reform begin. It started at the monastery of Cluny, in southern France. There the monks, inspired by strong religious faith, began to institute the moral reform of the clergy, restoring general obedience to Christian moral precepts, especially the vows of poverty and celibacy. But the Cluny reform movement becomes significant and gains momentum when the German rulers, whose power like that of the French and other European rulers was eroding with feudalism, attempt to counteract the disintegration that threatened them.

Before feudalism, titles of nobility — dukes, counts, margraves, etc. — were administrative positions under the Emperor. Those who were thus appointed were charged with carrying out the will of the central imperial authority in outlying districts. As fragmentation grew, these nobles began to assert themselves as sovereigns in their own right. They broke away from the central authority, appointed their own successors, eventually making the title and its powers hereditary.

New difficulties arose when the same property was claimed by a number of heirs. To counteract the fragmentation brought about by more than one son inheriting, *primogeniture* was introduced, giving the eldest son sole right to the title and all that went with it. This, in turn, brought on further difficulties: states were broken up by wars; younger sons rebelled; and where the bishops were powerful, they could forbid primogeniture and keep the temporal rulers weak.

To stem the process of disintegration and the difficulties it produced, the German Emperor appointed as his ministers, whenever he could, members of the clergy, encouraging, at the same time, the Cluny reforms. These Imperial appointees, sworn to celibacy, could have no heirs; and even if in the course of their administration they acquired greater power by wars or donations, all of it, when they died, reverted to the Emperor. By this ingenious plan, the Emperor built up his power in Germany. He then turned to Italy, using the Cluny reforms successfully for a similar purpose.

In Rome, the Pope had been controlled by contending petty nobles from the fall of Charlemagne to the 10th century. He was elected by the local clergy with the consent of the Roman population which, in turn, was dominated by the petty nobility. When the German Emperor Henry III thought he had the power to do so, he descended into Italy and broke the control of the Roman nobles. This was followed by the installation of German Popes, who adhered to the Cluny reforms.

The Emperor of course was looking after his own interests; but his tyrannic move had a healthy effect on the clergy. During his reign, he appointed four German popes, but the main focus of ecclesiastical reform during this time was a Cluny monk called Hildebrand. He had been appointed by the clergy, with the consent of the Emperor, to be the spiritual director of the reform movement in Rome. A supremely religious man with no aspirations for high office, he was dedicated to reforming the Church in the spirit of Christ. He had a realistic understanding of the problems involved in Church reform and Church management but also saw the dangers in the Emperor's interest in Church reform. Although that interest had served well thus far, he began, while an advisor to the popes appointed by Henry III, to institute a reform that had as its final end the separation of the Church from imperial authority and influence.

When Hildebrand assumed the Papacy himself, he quickly made known his intention to free the Church from imperial domination. As Gregory VII, he initiated the great struggle against Henry IV, who succeeded his father Henry III to the imperial throne — the struggle Dante describes in the dramatic masque at the top of Purgatorio. The fight was taken up by the Emperors who followed: Frederick I (Barbarossa), Frederick II, Manfred, the young Conradin, and of course Henry VII. After Gregory II, the Papal side was taken up by Innocent III, Innocent IV, and Boniface VIII — all immortalized in Dante's great poem.

The struggle took many turns and sometimes, in the heat of battle, the contestants on either side made unreasonable demands. At first the popes attempted merely to have the right to judge the moral qualifications of the rulers, to determine whether or not they were fit Christians; but enraged by imperial opposition they went so far as to claim that the Emperor received his temporal authority from the Church. Against this assertion, the imperial party claimed that, as an anointed Christian ruler, the Emperor had spiritual as well as temporal power, that anointment made him a religious leader on a par with the Pope himself — superior to him, in fact, since the Emperor also had legitimate temporal power, derived from God. Some Emperors went so far as to claim that the Pope had spiritual authority only by virtue of the Emperor's consent, for the Emperor corresponded to God the Father and the Pope to God the Son.

At first, the Emperor had the advantage. Frederick II, building on the victories of his grandfather, Barbarossa, made such rapid conquests wherever he went that it seemed as though he would soon recover control of an Empire almost as vast as that of Charlemagne. The Church meanwhile was trying to rally as much strength o its side as it could and resorted not only to spiritual means, such as excommunication, but to outright force, calling upon lesser rulers to fight in the name of the Church against the attacks of the Emperor. It was as though a mother were to appeal to one of her sons to defend her against the father who has become over-dominating and tyrannical. The Church appealed for help to the kings of France and to some of the communes of central and northern Italy. The French kings agreed for reasons of their own: they took the occasion to set up a monarchy in central Italy, at the expense of the Emperor. The Italian communes, Florence especially, joined in to win temporal gains and build up their trade also at the expense of the Emperor. Eventually the Church won out. Frederick's bastard son, Manfred, was defeated by Charles of Anjou in league with the Italian communes, and the attempts of the young Conradin to regain imperial authority were frustrated with his death as a "war criminal," the first example in the Western world of such a trial and execution at the hands of a victorious army.

The Empire was defeated but the Church did not enjoy its victory for long. Once the father was gone, the sons who had been called in to defend their mother became even more tyrannical and arrogant and abusive. The fight between father and mother, between the Empire and the Church, had been so drawn out and violent that when it was all over the Church, thoroughly exhausted, was no match for the growing sons, for whom the struggle had served to strengthen their muscles. The communes and the French King soon turned against the Church, anticipating a new obstacle in their way, and made her submit to their demands. The French King, Philip IV, actually forced the Pope from Rome to Avignon, where the Vicar of Christ would serve, in effect, as the King's chaplain.

Dante, offended like so many others by the outcome of the struggle — the Empire broken and the Pope a virtual prisoner at the French Court — offered a plan that might bring about peace in the Christian family, restoring the mother to her proper role and the father to his, so that the children, who looked to them for protection and guidance, could feel secure. He was no means the first to formulate a program for intelligent management of the Christian family: St. Paul had offered suggestions, Tertullian and St. Augustine and Pope Gelasius and many others down to St. Thomas, had offered plans. To understand what is peculiarly new in Dante's, we must look at what he derived from his predecessors.

We must remember that Dante's attitude toward the problem of human conduct, temporal and spiritual, is not an isolated subject; it involves the entire medieval world picture. This holds for Shakespeare as well. Most literary historians agree that the main body of European literature — from Dante and Petrarch and Chaucer and Spenser and Shakespeare and Milton, right down to Goethe's *Faust,* and the literature of the 19th century — can only be properly understood against the background of the medieval world picture. And the first thing to note is that the medieval world picture is an *ethical* one. There have been other kinds of world pictures. Ours in America is a scientific one, emphasizing physical laws. We think of whirling atoms, of the universe in terms of expanding galaxies. We have ethical concepts concerning the behavior of men and women, but we do not look at the whole universe ethically. We look at it scientifically, to see what it *is* not what it ought to be. Other ages have formulated what must be called an epistemological world picture; the Germans philosophers and poets of the 19th century pictured the universe in that way.

In building up a world picture, an American might ask: What are the facts of nature? A German philosopher might begin with: How do we come to know anything? The medieval thinkers began by asking: How ought things to be? How ought a man to behave? This kind of questions implies a finalistic purpose in things, a conception alien to a German epistemological view or the modern scientific view. Medieval men assumed that all things had a purpose. Modern science since Galileo and Bacon and Newton has said: Whether or not things have a purpose remains to be seen: we cannot assume it. Dante assumed that all things in the universe, from the meanest worm or particle of dust to the lofty stars, had a purpose and that all things were directed toward one universal goal or end. All things operated together in harmony toward that end.

The first and basic question they asked was: What ought an individual do in life? How should he behave as a human bring? The question is still a vital one, for us as well as Dante. It isn't a question we ask immediately. When we're born things are done for us, we don't ask any questions. Eventually we're encouraged to do things for ourselves; sometimes we act on our own, spontaneously, for reasons we don't understand. Before we get around to asking an ethical question about ourselves, about life, we've absorbed, like a sponge, a lot of experience. We have been acting long before we get around to asking a question about how we ought to act. In fact, before we ever phrase that kind of question, we have already learned many answers to it. Our parents and other mature relatives have repeatedly told us how we ought to act; our friends expect certain things from us. We begin to sift those demands only when they seem to conflict with one another. Who do you listen to then?

The men of Dante's time said: Let's see what others before us have said in trying to solve this problem. They applied the Baconian method to ethics long before Bacon was born. They compiled books containing the observations of as many learned men as they could find, *books of sentences* (as they were called), which provided a kind of introductory chapter to any serious thought on ethics. These books served as great encyclopedias, recording conveniently hundreds and hundreds of observations on the problem of human conduct. Like Bacon later, the schoolmen of the middle ages did not think it possible for an individual, counting on his own limited resources, to settle any matter intelligently. Like Bacon, they believed that men should pool their knowledge. The *books of sentences*, these encyclopedic compilations of "sayings," of facts and observations, were the pooled resources. They were built around questions arranged with *pros* and *cons*, thousands of questions of every sort and thousands and thousands of pros and cons. How thoroughly investigated these questions were is attested up to our very day. The great atheists of our time still do what Voltaire did when he wanted to get information to refute arguments of the Church: they turn to these *books of sentences* and find in the pros and cons more than enough material for their purpose — indeed, more than they could ever think up for themselves. Their main sources were the compilations of Isidorus of Seville and Peter Lombard, but there are many others.

With these compilations to stimulate and guide them, the medieval schoolmen were able to proceed toward answers. They argued first: you have to know what man is. Well, to know what man we have to distinguish him from other things. To do that, one must know what other things are. This is still the method of scientific definition today: relate a thing to all other things in nature in order to understand what that particular thing is. In the same way, the medievalists formulated their ethical questions into a world picture.

What is man? He is a heavy body first of all. Like a stone, he has weight and tends to fall, if nothing holds him up. But he's not just a solid body. There are liquids in him, blood, digestive juices, etc. There's air that he breathes in and out and fire that keeps his body at an even warm temperature, like a furnace heats a house regardless of the temperature outside. He is a compound of elements — but that's just the beginning. He's also capable of growth and reproduction, like a plant. He is also capable of perceiving — of seeing and hearing, smelling and tasting and touching — like animals. Still a compound of elements capable of growing and reproducing that perceives and moves is not necessarily a man. Even if one adds passions to such a creature, love and hate, that doesn't make it human, for animals also have passions. And so, the schoolmen concluded that man is not simply an element or a compound of elements, or a plant or an animal: what defines them does not define him.

There are other things man is not. He is not an idea or a thought. Man is embodied and thought is not. And yet, he contains thoughts and ideas. He is not like the thought of a house or a pot, yet he is capable of thinking of a house or pot. He can even design with his mind a house and a pot; he can materialize them even, actually build a house or a pot. Similarly, although he can contain ideas of works of art, religion, and philosophy, he is not those in himself. Such ideas can exist in him, but they are not part of him like his stomach or his arms. Such ideas, moreover, are not exclusively his. The very same ideas can exist in other people. You can have the same ideas of art or of God, or of society, as I have, so in a very true sense ideas are separable from us in a way that the parts of our body are not. My arm is my arm, but my idea of an arm is very likely the same as yours. Still, man is not an idea any more than he a compound of elements or a plant or an animal.

Yet all of these things are in man. He is not a plant, yet there are the essentials of a plant in him. He is not immaterial, like the idea of Justice, yet such ideas are in him. And since *material* and *immaterial* are opposites, we may conclude that that man is made up of opposites, of embodied and disembodied things. Embodied things, like his arm or liver, are his alone; other things, like disembodied ideas, exist as much in him as in the next man. The schoolmen expressed all this with a phrase as basic as Socrates's "know thyself" or Descartes's "I think, therefore I am" or the "Liberty, Equality, and Fraternity" of the French Revolution, or Woodrow Wilson's "Save the world for democracy," or President Roosevelt's "four freedoms." The phrase that dominated the thought of 1,000 years was "Mankind is the horizon."

Man is the point of contact or rather the line of contact between the sphere of the material — elements, compounds, plants and animals — and the sphere of the immaterial, where ideas reside. He is the material thing that tends to be full of ideas. No other material thing, no particle of dust, no compound of elements, no plant, no other animal shares ideas with man. Or, put another way: the "idea" of a stone is to fall towards the center of the earth. The "idea" of liquids is to flow at a uniform level. The "idea" of air is to settle above the earth and water; of fire, to rise. The "idea" of plants is to reproduce and grow; the "idea" of animals it to perceive and move eagerly toward or fearfully away from things, in response to their passions. Man has all these things in common with material things, but he also has the ability to *think* about them — and much else. He thinks about everything: his sexual desires, his hunger and what it means to be hungry, about what he wants and what he fears.

Thinking about his passions is what separates man from other animals, but it doesn't stop there. A man who thinks only about eating, about how he can get the most pleasure out of eating, even though he may make a pig of himself (as the saying goes), is still a man. Those who can think of nothing else but sex are still human beings. The process of *thinking*, howsoever applied, is what characterizes a human being. Birds build nests and catch worms, beavers dam rivers, bees build complicated honeycombs, man thinks as well as acts.

His thinking can go beyond eating or sex or clothing and sheltering his body. He can go beyond his needs and passions to think about the future, reconstruct the past, think about the stars and the heavens, and he can also think about the process of thought itself. When a man reaches that point, he enters a new arena. *Why* do I think about eating, about sex, about all those other things?

What is *thought*? What is the object of thinking? The serious men of the middle ages answered: the nature of man is to think, just as the nature of a stone is to fall, the nature of a plant to grow and reproduce. The nature of man is to think, which means: having thought about the things and objects around him, he can then turn to thinking about his nature, his *tendency to think.*

Passions tend to distract man from realizing that full potential. Some men can think of nothing else but satisfying their hunger, or their sexual appetites, or their other cravings. Left to fend for himself in a forest, a man might think of nothing else but self-preservation, how to get out of there as quickly as possible. He might then turn to finding ways of simplifying life by division of labor. His offsprings might be taught quickly what they have learned. The schoolmen argued that until man had satisfied most of his material needs, he could not be expected to give his attention to what the final object of his thinking might be. It is a task no single individual can expect to accomplish alone, no one generation even.

Indeed, many generations are needed to reach that end. Men have done much, so far, said the schoolmen. From Socrates and Plato, through Aristotle and the stoics, men have come to know much about what is peculiar to man. Moreover, they have been greatly helped by God, who in His divine dictates, the Holy Scriptures, has explained, in words that even the basest among us can understand, the object of human thought. It is the same as Plato's and Aristotle's: to know the absolute truth, absolute good and beauty, absolute power. The way of the philosophers is hard, the way of Scriptures easy, but the end is the same.

Why is the way of the philosopher hard? The schoolmen answered: fallen nature. Before the fall, man tended toward absolute truth naturally, easily, just like fire tends to rise by nature and a stone to fall. Man lost that natural tendency with the fall from grace, and since then has been tangled up in his animal passions, his material needs. Few have come anywhere near finding their way out of that entanglement.

The possibility to do so came with Christian revelation. It provided man with the means for restoring his pristine nature. Faith in Christ would allow him to orient himself in this world. With faith, material purpose is transformed into a spiritual one, and man is able to recognize that the object of living is to see the highest truth and power and beauty and goodness: to know God.

In the 13th century, most men were faithful Christians: a good beginning. Having recovered through the sacrifice of Christ the natural footing he had lost through Adam's fall, man could now turn to the serious business of social organization, division of labor, education of future generations, defense against enemies. Under the guidance of Christ's Church, he could do this more effectively than ever before.

At the same time that the great struggle between Church and Empire was taking place, St. Thomas formulated a scheme of social organization — the relationship of church and society — which has remained the official conception of the Roman Catholic Church. The design called for one universal church and many nations. He argued thus: Why do men live in organized society? The answer is: men need one another in order to satisfy their needs. They are instinctively gregarious, tend to join together in an organized society to insure their material well-being. This need holds the family together, holds the tribe, the village, the town together. At some point, as Aristotle had taught, when enough men are gathered together to supply all their material needs, the gregarious instinct is no longer felt and a qualitative change takes place: the community becomes self-sufficient, materially, both in man-power and resources.

Self-sufficiency was what Aristotle termed that qualitative change that distinguished a state from a lesser aggregate of people. Aristotle held that men held together naturally only until they reached a state of self-sufficiency. Any joining of men over and beyond what is necessary for self-sufficiency was unnatural. St. Thomas adopted this view. A universal empire, One World, is unnatural on a material basis. It was natural only on a spiritual basis. He argued that since governments are naturally organized for material or temporal well-being, they ought naturally to be many, because material well-being can be satisfied when enough men are gathered together to preserve themselves against attack. When one nation attempts to dominate others, those others will naturally be obliged to band together to defend themselves against the aggressor; but when the aggressor is beaten, that obligation will not longer hold. Men living in peace tend to break down into self-sufficient units, in which social organization is maintained with the minimum red tape and the least expense. A big nation has a tremendous overhead, it becomes top-heavy; a community has its own immediate administration in the city, then it must send and pay delegates to the state congresses, then to the Federal congress, and so on. This is expensive. When there is peace, when there is no threat, the tendency is to economize, to enjoy low taxes, low overhead government costs. The ideal is: what is enough for self-sufficiency.

This had been the experience of the city-states of

Greece, which had banded together against the Persians but fell to fighting among themselves when there was no more threat. Alexander's Empire broke up because it was hard to hold together. So did the Roman Empire. So did Charlemagne's. The separate nations banded together with the Italian communes to fight the German emperor, and when he was defeated the communes set to fighting among themselves once more. Modern examples are legion. Think only of the United States and Russia, allied in the fight against Fascism but after defeating the common enemies back to fighting each other tooth and nail in a "cold war."

St. Thomas believed that it would take more than temporal interests to make *one* united humanity. It would take worship of God, adherence to that supreme value. And since the emperor himself conceded that worship of God was administered not by the State but by the Church, let all men be united as one in the Church and divided according to their temporal needs. Furthermore, to make sure that the temporal needs are subordinated to spiritual needs, let the Church have the last word in quarrels between Church and State.

Dante accepted this general picture, with one distinction. He had no quarrel with the ethical questions raised earlier or the definitions of spiritual and temporal needs. He accepted the notion that temporal ends should be subordinated to spiritual ends, that the attainment of spiritual heavenly happiness was more important than the attainment of peace and happiness on earth; but he did not agree with Aristotle or St. Thomas that temporal rule based on temporal needs must always result in a plurality of states. His ideas for *one* world, on world government, have been given a lot of publicity in recent years by people who also believed that one world was the answer to wars and nationalism.

Dante held to that ideal, even as he witnessed its failure. The great struggle between the Universal Church and the Universal Empire ended in the destruction of both and the rise of national units, new monarchies, each jealous of its own possessions, anxious to expand, ready to fight one another at the slightest provocation. The Church whose business it was to look after the spiritual well-being of all humanity was not functioning as it should; it was being held captive in Avignon. Everywhere there was fighting and moral disorder. According to Dante, things had never been so bad. All you saw was nation against nation, city against city, neighborhood against neighborhood, family against family, even brother against brother (as he tells us in the *Commedia*). What has become of Christian unity, of Christian life? Living has become so violent that men can hardly get beyond keeping alive as animals, much less find their way to their proper spiritual ends.

What's the reason for such disorder? he asks. Who's to blame? His answer is: the Church. If the Roman Catholic Church had tended to its own spiritual business instead of interfering with the temporal business of the emperor, the world would not be in the sorry state in which it now finds itself. There would be peace and moral order instead of chaos, a world in which men could study and carry on the serious business of human life, which is to acquire knowledge of the highest truth, the highest good, the highest beauty, the highest love: the study of God.

Dante never forgets the ultimate end of man, his fulfillment in heaven, and in this respect, he belongs to the middle ages. He is essentially modern in subscribing to the belief that attainment of peace and happiness on earth is a prerequisite for the attainment of man's ultimate spiritual end — a short step from the argument of modern humanitarians that universal peace is the supreme end of man. Dante himself never reached that point; but the notion took root within 25 years of his death: with Petrarch and Boccaccio we are out of the middle ages and in the modern age.

Dante's idealism was not an empty dream; it was rooted in a profound belief that in their present state men were greedy, selfish, and self-serving. Only the Emperor who had everything and wanted nothing and the spiritual leader in Rome who took his job seriously could effect a change. The end proclaimed by Virgil could not be realized by the Romans, for they knew nothing about the Christian dispensation and Christ; but a Christian Emperor could reach that end and, together with the Vicar of Rome, bring peace and order to the world, or, in Virgil's words, "raise the oppressed and crush the aggressors of the world," showing mankind the true path to happiness.

A NOTE ON TRANSLATING DANTE

Based on a review in Western Humanities Review, XXXIV, Number 2 (1980) of Dante's Rime, translated by Patrick S. Diehl, (Princeton University Press, 1979).

A new collection of Dante's *Rime* with facing English translations is indeed welcome. Professor Diehl has undertaken an ambitious project and deserves credit. Anyone who has spent time on *stilnovist* poetry knows that — aside from the usual frustrations every translator must learn to live with — the compressed, fluent, and deceptively simple language of poets like Guido Guinicelli, Guido Cavalcanti, and Dante himself (more direct in many ways and more "contemporary" in syntax and vocabulary than, say, the great 19th romantic poet of Italy, Giacomo Leopardi) is virtually impossible to reproduce in English so as to retain the organic complex of sound, meaning, image clusters, and disciplined diction which characterizes that unusual poetry. The difficulty is compounded when a translator is tempted to set up priorities that undermine even his best efforts.

Professor Diehl sets down his priorities very clearly in his Introduction:

> Dante's rhyme-schemes and line-lengths have been faithfully reproduced, even in the sonnet exchanges, where the correspondents will deliberately choose the rarest and most difficult rhyme-sounds in order to make the task of duplicating them in the reply all the more arduous. . . . The translator must embrace the technical demands of his task as a magnificent opportunity; to flinch from them would be fatal to this poetry. . . . To pursue such a course puts considerable pressure on English idiom and syntax. . . . The reader must judge how far I have succeeded in resisting this pressure.

To maintain Dante's line-lengths is indeed possible and the effort commendable, but to insist on Dante's rhyme-schemes is another matter. Trying to find English equivalents for Dante's rhyme sequences is indeed a bold challenge; even "the rarest and most difficult rhyme-sounds" of the sonnet exchanges are relatively easy compared with what is available in rhyming word endings in English. A more worthy effort might have been to focus on meaning and linguistic fluency, even at the expense of the rhyme-scheme.

To maintain his line-lengths, Professor Diehl often resorts to esoteric words (Pound also did, but they worked better for him) or to images not in the original (Rossetti also did, and destroyed the smooth transparency of the Italian). The result is often heavy and awkward. The need to fill the line in English to correspond with the Italian line-length also produces confusion at times, especially when words not in the original are introduced to create the programmed result. These priorities more often than not destroy the Italian syntactical structure and obscure meaning.

Number 15 (pp. 48-49) might be cited as an illustration of what has been said thus far. The language of the original is remarkably limpid and simple. Without any trimmings, the first stanza of the poem might read in English (my translation):

> Guido, I wish that you and Lapo and I
> Could be swept up as if by magic
> And put down in a ship that turned with every wind
> According to your whims and mine. . . .

Professor Diehl's translation reads:

> Guido, I wish that you and Lapo and I
> Were taken up by strong ensorcelment
> And set in ship, whatever winds were sent.
> Who'd go the way we chose (no matter why). . . .

Professor Diehl's translation of Number 41 (pp. 84-85) doesn't read badly at first glance:

> Mistress Dejection came to me one day
> And sitting down, said this: "I've come to bide."
> And as it seemed, she brought on either side
> Sorrow and Gloom as comrades for the stay.
>
> And I said to her: "Get up and go away,"
> And she gave answer with a Grecian's pride. . . .

The need to rhyme turns what is beautifully fluent in the Italian into something quaint at best, in English.

The Italian, simply translated, goes like this:

One day. Melancholy found her way to me
And said: I want to stay with you a while";
And with her she brought, it seemed to me,
Sorrow and Rage to keep her company.

And I said to her: Go on, now; go away";
And she answered like a Greek. ... .

In this particular case, the phrase Grecian's pride — "pride" to rhyme with "aside" in the next line and with bide" and "side" in the previous stanza — makes little sense. To answer like a Greek suggests their notorious art of deception (cf. Ulysses in Canto XXVI of Inferno) and would be a more likely reference here.

Dante's stringent imagistic constructions should take precedence over any attempt at rhyme. The special language of the *stilnovists* — like the language of the metaphysical poets — is charged with philosophical suggestions. Such verbs as "vertù," "valore," "luce," "raggio," "cosa bella," "diletto," "mente," "ragione," "ragionando," "signoria," "nobiltà," "gentile," "occhi," "risplende," "foco," "fiamma," etc. are almost always part of an image-cluster that should be maintained in translation. They are words subtly or explicitly woven together to suggest the constant search for psychological equivalents for the physiological state brought about by love. The mysterious effect of love on both the body and soul is, moreover, intimately connected with a Platonic "given" which begins with the attraction to beauty, moves on to the desire to possess beauty, and resolves finally in the identity with beauty. The trick is to keep the deceptive simplicity of this special language without destroying the precision of the large premise which sustains it poetically.

Professor Diehl tries to retain that special language in his translation but, again, the need for rhyme forces him very often to dilute the effect of the "core" words. In the second stanza of Number 67 (pp. 112-113), "luce" is translated "lucidity," and "come raggio in stella" becomes "like stars with sunlight stayed" — when all Dante says is "your light is always in my heart

/ like rays [are always] in a star. . . . In Number 69 (pp. 132-134), Dante's "È gentilezza dovunqu'è vertute, / ma non vertute ov'ella . . ." is translated "Nobility is found in virtue's sphere / but she holds more by far. . . ." "L'anima cui adorna esta bontate / non la si tiene ascosa," is translated "The soul who takes this goodness as her gauge / won't hide it from the light"; and on pp. 134-135: "e sua persona adorna di bieltade / con le sue parti accorte" becomes "and beauty walks beside her as her page / with all that suits her best."

In some cases, the lines have errors that cannot be excused even in the light of the priorities the translator has chosen to follow. In translating "Vedete omai quanti son l'ingannati!" ("See how many have been deceived [or misled]," Professor Diehl gives the key word, "ingannati," a totally different meaning from Dante's and in so doing creates confusion with, "How many wanderers need to hear these rhymes!"

Perhaps none.